DEVELOPING LITERACY SKILLS ACROSS THE CURRICULUM

Front Cover Graphic by Jeanette Moss.

DEVELOPING LITERACY SKILLS ACROSS THE CURRICULUM
Practical Approaches, Creative Models, Strategies, and Resources

Edited by
Loretta Walton Jaggers
Nanthalia W. McJamerson
and
Gwendolyn M. Duhon

Mellen Studies in Education
Volume 60

The Edwin Mellen Press
Lewiston•Queenston•Lampeter

LIBRARY
FRANKLIN PIERCE COLLEGE
RINDGE. NH 03461

Library of Congress Cataloging-in-Publication Data

Developing literacy skills across the curriculum : practical approaches, creative models, strategies, and resources / edited by Loretta Walton Jaggers, Nanthalia W. McJamerson, Gwendolyn M. Duhon.
    p. cm. -- (Mellen studies in education ; v. 60)
    Includes bibliographical references and index.
    ISBN 0-7734-7469-2
    1. Language arts--Correlation with content subjects--United States. 2. Interdisciplinary approach in education--United States. 3. Curriculum planning--United States. I. Jaggers, Loretta Walton. II. McJamerson, Nanthalia W. III. Duhon, Gwendolyn M. IV. Series.

  LB1576 .D453 2001
  428'.0071--dc21

                                00-069056

This is volume 60 in the continuing series
Mellen Studies in Education
Volume 60 ISBN 0-7734-7469-2
MSE Series ISBN 0-88946-935-0

A CIP catalog record for this book is available from the British Library.

Copyright © 2001 The Edwin Mellen Press

All rights reserved. For information contact

The Edwin Mellen Press
Box 450
Lewiston, New York
USA 14092-0450

The Edwin Mellen Press
Box 67
Queenston, Ontario
CANADA L0S 1L0

The Edwin Mellen Press, Ltd.
Lampeter, Ceredigion, Wales
UNITED KINGDOM SA48 8LT

Printed in the United States of America

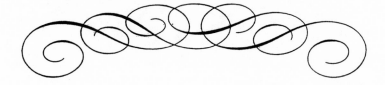

Table of Contents

Preface

The development of literacy skills across the curriculum focuses on ways of enhancing learning through the use of a variety of creative techniques and approaches. Information is presented on collaboration with administrators, teachers, the home, community and other school personnel. The ideas discussed in the book underscore the longstanding and pedagogically significant point in literacy education, "that the integrated approach in teaching is basic to fundamental learning." This approach supports the idea that the sorts of words needed in one subject area are also used or will extend understanding in other subject areas in the curriculum. The key emphasis here is and has been to read with understanding enhances concept formation.

Developing literacy skills across the curriculum is an integrated approach, which will ensure that our children, the future leaders of this nation, are literate. They must be able to read, write, possess knowledge and be well informed. For earlier directions on teaching children to read, educators were greatly influenced by reports of the National Committee on reading instruction. William S. Gray chaired the committee, whose leading publications were in the twenties and thirties, 1925 and 1937.

Over time, it has become obvious or experientially clear that while reading is the key to learning, reading is more than merely calling words. Reading is the process of bringing meaning to the printed page. When one pronounces words and there is no picture in the readers mind, no meaningful concepts are formed. A truism is that "reading is bringing meaning to the printed page."

The collaborative approach to developing literacy skills presented in this book provides a variety of opportunities for students to expand their concepts. They are able to incorporate their background of experiences and interests in broad, unique learning activities as they study different subjects in the curriculum. The different strategies presented for developing literacy skills across the curriculum are designed to enhance the development of concepts through the emphasis on the integrated approach in learning; in education. The obvious and meaningful connection between the teaching of reading, writing, as well as other subjects in the curriculum, is becoming widely recognized as the best approach for expanding the literacy skills of students.

Helen Richards-Smith, Ph.D.,
Dean,
Earl Lester Cole Honors College
Grambling State University

CHAPTER 1

Enhancing Academic Achievement Through A
Continuum of Literacy Activities

Mrs. Evelyn S. Francois
Mrs. Wanda F. Randall
New Orleans Public Schools
New Orleans, LA

Dr. Neari F. Warner
Grambling State University
Grambling, LA

This chapter is designed to demonstrate that academic achievement can be enhanced greatly if literacy skills and activities are promoted throughout the educational continuum. The chapter uses a large, urban public school system as the experiential base to discuss activities and strategies that promote achievement from K - 12. It will describe creative methods that promote literacy skills and develop positive attitudes for reading and writing. The chapter will also discuss the challenge of promoting literacy in higher education institutions.

In this new millennium, educators will continue to face a multiplicity of challenges. Included among the many challenges are those brought by students: those who are not interested in school, those whose self-esteems are very low, those whose mores and values are inconsistent with what is expected in the school setting, and those whose drive and motivation to succeed in school are minimal. The task of educators, then, is to attempt to overcome all of the aforementioned obstacles and create a positive teaching/learning environment that will motivate students to their highest level of excellence.

Where there is potential, it is important that school systems connect with parents as early as possible to engage their involvement. Through parent groups, structured and unstructured, school systems should attempt to apprise parents of the important role they play in school achievement. Statistics have proved that parental involvement greatly improves children's achievement as well as their desire to succeed. There is no doubt that early parental involvement in students' educational activities has a lasting effect throughout their matriculation in educational settings.

Nonetheless, as students enter formal school settings, there will be many who have had little or no early parental involvement. Notwithstanding the reality of this, teachers are expected to demand high achievement from all students. As such, school systems nationwide are demanding more rigorous academic standards for K-12 students. Standard-based reform has become the benchmark for schools. Feldman (1999) posits that setting high standards and making schools and students accountable for reaching them will raise the achievement of all children. This is the vision- the ideal goal of each teacher. However, the inherent difficulty in achieving high levels of accountability is compounded by the large number of students whose achievement levels meet minimum standards or whose skill levels are basic at best. In many classrooms, a disproportionate number of students need additional assistance to master the skills of effective reading and writing. Correspondingly, teachers everywhere are saying that as students need more help, they, too, need help and better training, extended instruction time for students, a sustained effort that they, the children, and their parents can count on (Feldman, 1999).

The large urban school system, which supports the information of this chapter, has attempted a variety of strategies and activities to enhance teachers' success, to motivate students, to raise their levels of achievement, and to heighten their awareness of the importance of acquiring good literacy skills. Within these activities, several outcomes have been noted, including (1) training for teachers has been provided; (2) students have received creative and innovative activities; and (3) collaboration among parents and communities has been achieved. Statewide, teachers understand that they will be the ones to inspire students to excel and to make application of their learning to real life experiences (Reaching for Results, 1998).

3

Toward this end, one strategy required teachers to give up fifteen minutes of their daily free time to assist students. This also allowed the school to have early dismissal two days out of each month. These days were used as Professional Development Inservices. During these times, the faculty and staff discussed new trends and strategies that would help to improve student learning and strengthen the classroom environment. Resource personnel from the central office were brought in to provide informational seminars and hands-on workshops. The focus of all sessions was to better train teachers to meet the needs of the students. Relatedly, the central office distributed a bi-monthly publication, The K - 3 Initiator, to keep teachers informed of new and developing practices.

Special literacy-focused activities are other ways of communicating and supporting teachers in their quest to help improve student learning. For example, A Reading and Math Summit will always help a faculty, particularly in schools that are highly populated with low-achieving students. The purpose of the summit must be to discuss and concentrate on preparing students to become strategic readers and problem-solvers (K-3 Initiator, 1999). Motivational speakers, panel discussions and impromptu respondents from faculties in neighboring communities and school systems will also provide a wealth of information and insight. Idea-sharing among peers is an invaluable interactive tool that produces camaraderie and support for teachers who often shoulder the blame for underachievement in their schools.

Teachers in these areas and these schools, labeled at-risk, realize that the literacy effort must be intense and continuous. Therefore, throughout the school year, including Saturdays, workshops are held. The sessions are designed to help teachers increase their knowledge base and creativity to ensure their abilities to deliver content for success. Teachers in the system are provided with a Teachers Center, which serves as a production area, as well as a place for them to secure resource and reference materials. Teachers frequent the Center to gain ideas and to prepare bulletin boards, manipulatives, games and other teaching/classroom materials. Workshops are also held at the Center. The Center is integral to the school system and has become the hub of information and activities for keeping teachers abreast of educational trends. The Center is provided to the teachers by an advocacy group, which promotes and supports teachers' issues and concerns and services the financial needs of its members.

In this state, by legislature statute, teaching students to read must be the highest priority. From a House bill during the regular session (R. S. 17:24:9), Louisiana provided for the development and the implementation of a quality, early reading and math initiative. Accordingly, teachers and school systems were mandated to develop a balanced and comprehensive approach to reading and mathematics in the primary grades, appropriately named K-3 Reading Initiative (Bulletin 1967). Thus, teachers in the school system had to become committed to developing independent, competent and avid learners.

A wide range of approaches, activities, strategies and programs geared toward students are being used to accomplish the mandate. Spring 1999 data from all public and elementary schools containing first, second and third grade show an increase in scores as a result of this initiative.

For many students, Project Read is very helpful (Greene, 1994). It is an alternative reading and writing program which provides a direct, systematic and multi-sensory approach where emphasis is placed on active participation and effective use of time. Louisiana has already begun reading instruction reforms through the joint initiatives of the State Legislature and the State Board of Education. The new K-3 Reading and Math Initiative and an earlier accountability system have paid off in improved test scores (Burke, 1999). Reading instruction is matched to the learning styles of the students, making it a preventive rather than a remedial program (Pupil Progression Plan, 1998-99). This is demanded through the Reading for Excellence Act. The state is also working with experts from the Center for the Improvement of Early Reading Achievement (CIERA) in partnership with state universities and regional educational service centers to ensure that districts and schools receive the help they need (Burke, 1999).

Another system-wide strategy that has proved helpful is cooperative grouping and cooperative learning. This is a successful teaching strategy in which small teams, each with students of different levels of ability, use a variety of learning activities to improve their understanding of a subject. (Education Research Consumer Guide, 1992). As indicated by its name, students work together in small groups to achieve a common goal. Positive interdependence, individual accountability, and development of social skills are some of the benefits of this strategy. It also promotes higher achievement, increases self-esteem and improves attitudes towards school and learning. Having been used for many years, Learning Centers continue to be useful in motivating students. These areas of organized learning materials are used to reinforce learning as well as to introduce new material. Equally important, they enable students to take responsibility for their own learning destinies.

The national project DEAR (Drop Everything And Read) is being implemented system-wide with much success. The flexibility that each school is given in determining the time and length of the program as well as the school's ability to decide whether the reading will be silent or aloud allows the school to take ownership of and pride in its program of sustained reading. Similarly, journal writing is being implemented across the system. Students at the schools write each day for fifteen minutes. They are instructed to put their thoughts, ideas and reflections into a special notebook. It was discovered that after their initial resistance, students began to look forward to expressing themselves in their own special ways. Notwithstanding the merit of each of these strategies, in the K - 6 schools, one method will not be the answer. There is no panacea. Rather, a combination of activities and strategies will more likely produce high achievement and a greater appreciation for reading and writing.

As with most school systems, this system operates on the premise that everyone must be involved in creating a learning environment for students. In this system librarians play an active role in the development of literacy skills and in cultivating an appreciation for language and literature. Programs and strategies that are being used by librarians reflect a change in the traditional, stereo-typed professional. It is also indicative of what the school system has judged as important. In concert with this, librarians/media specialists are components of the continuum.

8

Librarians are committed to equipping students with the necessary skills to do well on information literacy portions of the state mandated assessment. They also attempt to assist students in: expressing themselves intelligently, reacting to a variety of situations., writing reflectively on a miscellany of subjects, locating and using resources and transferring knowledge from one subject area to another.

A very popular library initiative is READ-IN. This project, closely aligned to the national program DEAR, is one in which everyone in the school stops whatever is being done and reads. This includes administrators, teachers, students, cafeteria workers, custodians and even visitors to the school site. The activity has become such an enjoyable experience that school personnel request the activity without provocation. However, in order for the activity to be effective, it should be done no more than three times a month. This is necessary to maintain interest, momentum and mystery. In anticipation of the event, student are asked to bring literature from home, or they may borrow from the Media Center or exchange books and news articles with classmates, This activity also fosters dialogue among students. Discussion time is given where students listen and react to their peers' opinion. This activity becomes a win-win situation for everyone. Students gain knowledge on a variety of subjects, and many who never took time to read for the sheer pleasure of reading seem to be enjoying it. Teachers prepare assignments from the project, and parents appear to love it based on the comments and expressions received.

The workshop, "Young Adult/Adolescent Literature: A Biobliotherapy Approach," is also a school librarian's initiative. The workshop centers on using literature as a means to gain insight into the minds of young adults and adolescents. It can also be used to explore and expand literacy by relying on specific books that young people can use to identify and align with their own lives. Students can relate outcomes and translate to make sound informed decisions. It is also a way to minister to the needs of youth by providing a blueprint of how youth in similar situations reached solutions and consensus in dealing with their problems.

Computer-based programs have gained much acceptance in schools systems. "The Accelerated Reader" is such a program. It allows students to read books at their pace, take computer-generated test, and write reactionary papers on the content. The computer tallies the score, provides thought-provoking questions, and even prints out a certificate of merit once the student has read a required number of volumes.

"Celebrity-Read-A-Thons" are also very popular in promoting literacy. Local television personalities, bank presidents, sports figures and others in the public eye join together to foster literacy. These activities help to underscore the advantages of a literate populace.

"Parents Read" is another fun activity whereby parents come into the school site to share a favorite book. Not only do they excerpt passages for oral reading, but they also discuss the implications and relevance of various themes. This program reinforces the significance of being an informed, thought-inspired member of the community.

The "Adopt-a-Book" project is also very parent and community centered. This project was designed to build dwindling library collections. Though started decades ago, the program is still current and popular. Parents and others are asked to donate specific volumes or to make financial contributions to purchase the volumes. Special bookplates are affixed to the books to identify the donor. As a result of this project, collections grew and continue to grow. This also sends a message about the importance of reading and having reading materials available.

In a related manner, this school system can spotlight the results of a focused, cohesive effort toward community/school literacy. One school, located in a depressed area of the city, boasts of having a public library housed within its walls. The students use the library and the community members use the library for their purposes. Many of these community persons were high school drop-outs who are now experiencing pride in themselves, in their children's school and in their community. This project has helped residents restructure their lives and their communities. This is a sterling example of how the educational continuum extends beyond the confines of the walls of a school building.

As students move into post secondary settings, the emphasis on literacy must be continued. However, it is important that colleges and universities implement a structure and a support system to promote continuing literacy development and appreciation. The system must begin as students enter the freshman year. Since freshman students do not automatically or magically adjust or adapt to the independence and self-sufficiency thrust upon them, their activities in literacy development should be guided. One strategy that universities can employ is providing incoming freshmen with reading lists. Concomitantly, there must be a designated class from which assignments will emanate and where structured discussions and testing will occur. To be successful, this strategy must be inextricably linked to some aspect of the student's academic curriculum.

Once students move beyond the freshman level, the challenge of engaging them in literacy activities may become more difficult. Upperclassmen are more likely to respond to activities that directly involve or impact their majors, their friendship circles and their social interests. Thus, trading groups and book clubs should be encouraged within the residence halls and in campus organizations. Book colloquia and symposia can best be cultivated from discipline and discipline-related subjects. The university library can sponsor a "Book of the Month" activity as well as technology-based projects that will attract students and test their imaginations and ingenuity.

Obviously, the university level presents the greatest challenge in the educational continuum of literacy activities. Nonetheless, it can happen and can be best facilitated if all segments of the university embrace the philosophy that literacy activities will enhance the academic social and cultural experiences of the students.

REFERENCES

Bulletin 1967, <u>Louisiana K-3 Reading and Math Initiative</u>, LA Department of Education.

Burke, J. (1999). LA Department of Education.

<u>Education Research Consumer Guide.</u> (1992, June).

Feldman, S. (May/June,1999). Making Standards Work. <u>American Teacher,</u> 93, 8.

Greene, V., & Enfield, M. (1994). <u>Phonology Guide,</u> Language Circle Enterprise.

<u>K - 3 Initiator</u>. (January, 1999). New Orleans Public Schools, No. 3.

Pupil Progression Plan, New Orleans Public Schools, 1998-99.

Reaching for Results. (November, 1998). Louisiana Education Reform, LA Department of Education, 1.

CHAPTER 2

Enhancing Literacy Skills and Self-Esteem of Minority Students Through Whole-Language and Literature

Gwendolyn M. Duhon, Ph.D.
McNeese State University
Lake Charles, LA

Katrina Boden-Webb, M. Ed.
Jimmy McJamerson, M.A. +68
Grambling State University
Grambling, LA

This article provides a definition and context for the concept of whole-language instruction. The whole-language approach to teaching reading is discussed and documentation is provided as to how students are positively impacted when reading stories about people from similar ethnic backgrounds and participating in activities that afford them opportunities to reflect and share their individual experiences. Sample lessons and literature using this approach will also be included.

There are various definitions or understandings about the concept of whole-language and whole-language instruction. It has at times been referred to as a program, a process, or a theory (Clark, 1994). Some studies conclude that no facile definition existed, that whole-language balanced skills and creativity, and that teachers' understandings evolved as they continued to adapt their classrooms to their students' needs (Gross & Shefelbine, 1991). Most succinctly, it is a set of beliefs about language, teaming, and literary. Its' basic tenants are that

1. all learning is social;

2. language is learned through use; and

3. purpose and intention drive learning (Clark, 1994).

Whole-language programs build upon a philosophy emphasizing the value of the reader's knowledge of language and experiences and active involvement in constructing meaning from print (Goodman, 1986). Combined language experiences that integrate reading and writing, individualized reading, literature units, and child-authored materials are educational practices that typify a language-centered reading approach (Zarillo, 1987).

Many traditional basal readers contain stories that tend to be far removed from the experiences of the readers and have little connection to real-life experiences. This is a major concern for minority students, who tend to find few commonalities with the characters and culture that is transmitted not only in the basals, but in many urban public schools in this country.

Children from minority and low income families enter school with different patterns of communication and participation than those expected and reinforced by the school, which reflect the practices and competencies of the majority society and are constituted to protect and reproduce those practices. Students who arrive at school with a different set of experiences and assumptions from those valued by the culture of the classroom are placed at disadvantages from the start (Davis, 1996).

By using a myriad of approaches that include using the readers' experiences as a context for understanding and responding to literature, whole language provides opportunities for success for minority students "who are struggling in a system which demands independence in literacy for school success-- yet which often fads to provide equal opportunities for that success" (Hollingsworth, Minarik, & Teel, 1990).

Whole-language allows students to take a more active role in the learning process by having them relate to the stories, their classmates, and even the teacher in new and innovative ways. Cooperative activities and student-authored materials create opportunities for students and teachers to respond to each other from positions of strengths, rather than engaging in the traditional process "of education in which those who know transmit specific knowledge to those who don't know" (Gross & Shefelbine, 1991). Through the whole-language activities and student-generated materials, many minority students find their voices and an outlet

17

for their untapped creativity. The students are engaged in activities that are meaningful, directly related to the stories, and can enhance their self-esteem and ethnic pride. They can see themselves and others like themselves in the literature, and can find ways to show their talents through the literature-related activities.

The following is an example how literature (poetry) can be used in whole-language instruction to teach concepts in language arts, mathematics, social studies, science, and music. The following poem was chosen because of the strong connection between pride, knowledge of history, and success. Furthermore the poem emphasizes all domains of education; cognitive, affective, and psychomotor, while enhancing the self-esteem of both male and female students. This poem and subsequent activities are geared for 8th grade students.

I Am "Bad", And You Can't Stop Me

I shall, I will excel because I am bad, and you cannot stop me. I read everything because knowledge is power. In math, the Pythagorean theorem is as easy as 1, 2, 3. 1 can recite the poetry of Nikki Giovanni with ease, and I can play Beethoven's 5th Symphony with the fortitude of my being. You see, I am naturally gifted that way, for I am bad, and you can't stop me.

I can run with the best runners, keeping stride with Flo Jo and Carl Lewis. I can soar with the eagles like Michael Jordan when he puts on his show, for I am bad and you cannot stop me.

I can achieve, and will achieve. My inspiration comes from the Nubian Queen-Tiye; Bilal-the Islamic crier; Kunta Kinte- who rejected slavery; Phyllis Wheatley- the first African-American poetess; Joe Louis- the "Brown Bomber"; Barbara Jordan- the superb warrior/lawyer; Marva Collins- the ultimate teacher; Sammy Davis, Jr. - the master showman; Dr. M. L. King- the supreme leader; and Jesse Jackson-the master politician. For I am bad and you cannot stop me.

Like Prince Hall- the father of Black Masonic life, like John Johnson of Ebony and Jet, I can achieve and I will achieve. Like Dr. Daniel Hale Williams, who performed the first successful open heart surgery or Dr. Benjamin Carson, a neurosurgeon, I can excel in medicine, too. For I am bad and you cannot stop me.

No drug pusher nor pimp can stop me; no racism, nor bigotry, nor injustice; for I am bad and you cannot stop me.

Like "Ice-T", I use my mind for a lethal weapon and like B.P.D. (Boogie Down Productions), I shall never forget my history, for I am bad and you cannot stop me.

Like Mohammed Ali, who declared, "I am the greatest ", I now declare, I am bad, and you cannot stop me!

Jimmy McJamerson
Copyright, 1990

LANGUAGE ARTS

Objective: To teach students to distinguish and understand denotative and connotative meanings of words.

Materials Needed: Dictionary

Using the terms "I Am Bad" and "...as "deep" as Malcolm X.", the teacher will discuss the meaning of the connotation (an implied meaning; a given meaning) and the denotation (dictionary meaning) of a word. The teacher will ask students to think of different meanings of the word "Bad". The teacher will write these meaning on the board. After discussion, the teacher should place words on the board that have both connotative and denotative meanings, e.g. *dense, rat, blue, cool, fly, sharp*, etc. Then, the class can be divided into pairs. Each pair is given a word to pantomime by the teacher. If needed, the students can look for the denotative

20

meaning of each word in the dictionary. Each pair is given the opportunity to pantomime for the class, one student pantomimes the connotative meaning of a word while the other student pantomimes the denotative meaning of the word. Using both pantomimes, the students should be able to guess which word the pair is pantomiming.

MATH

Objective: To teach students to use the Pythagorean Theorem

Materials: Counters to use as manipulatives, overhead projector

Using an overhead projector, the teacher after giving values for the variables "a", "b", and "c", can demonstrate the addition of the values and its sum. Furthermore, students can either work individually, in pairs, or as a cooperative group to demonstrate this concept. With the students sitting in pairs, a teacher can give the class three numbers to serve as values for the letters "a", "b", and "c". The teacher should make sure that the numbers are small enough so that the students will have enough counters to square all the numbers. The teacher would then have students to work along with him in their pairs as he uses his manipulatives on the overhead to demonstrate squaring each number and adding both "a" and "b". Afterwards, give each group three numbers to serve as values for the letters "a", "b", and "c". After students have

21

manipulated the counters to determine an answer, not necessary the right answer but an answer that pleases each group, the teacher would then have each pair to solve the problem using the overhead projector. Each pair will use their manipulatives at their desks to model the group that is presenting. After presentations, students should work additional problems using the Pythagorean Theorem on paper. Students may use counters, if needed.

Extension: This poem can be used to introduce a unit on triangles. The lessons can include the parts of triangles (lines, angles, legs, and hypotenuses), the types of triangles, types of angles, and the measurement of a triangle, as well as its angles and sides.

SOCIAL STUDIES

Objective: To compare and contrast the American Executive branch of government to the leader of an African tribal unit.

Materials: Weights of the same volume, balance beam the

After discussion and lecture of the duties and functions of the two leaders, the teacher should demonstrate that although the types of governments are different, the duties and responsibilities are the same, they are equal. One weight should be placed on each side of the balance beam for overall duties and/or responsibilities for each of the leaders, e.g. one weight each for governing the welfare of its people, one weight for each leader for solving the problems of its people, and so forth.

Extension: Either of the great achievers from this poem and their achievements can be discussed as social studies lessons. Tiye and Kunta Kinte can be great anticipatory sets for a unit on Africa. Dr. Martin Luther King, Jr. is a great person to begin a discussion on the Civil Rights movement or a study of the South during different periods of time. Furthermore, a unit can be developed on the three branches of government; the people that are involved in each branch, the reason for each branch, each branch's roles and responsibilities, and how people become qualified to serve on either branch.

SCIENCE

Objective: After discussion and class participation, the learner will be able to describe the heart and the position of the ventricles, atriums, and aorta and their functions.

Materials: Model or picture of the heart, stethoscope (can be borrowed from the school nurse) clay, straws, and markers.

As an anticipatory set, the students can be allowed to listen to their heartbeat through the stethoscope. After lecture and discussion, the students will be given a piece of clay, large enough to make a replica of the heart. The students should use the straws placed into the clay to demonstrate the location of the ventricles, atriums, and the aorta. The students should color the straws, having the straws representing the ventricles one color, the straws representing the atrium another color, and the aorta being one distinct color. Each model of the heart can be saved for use in other lessons relating to the heart.

Extension: Dr. Daniel Hale Williams opens the door for a unit on the circulatory system and/or organs of the body. Moreover, there may be detailed lessons about the heart, the functions of veins and arteries, and maintaining a healthy body.

CREATIVE ARTS - MUSIC
Objective: To introduce students to a variety of songs performed by Sammy Davis, Jr.
Materials: 3-4 songs that were performed by Sammy Davis, Jr.

The teacher can present information about the legendary Sammy Davis, Jr. After the presentation, students listen to a variety of his music and can discuss the types of songs that he performed.

In summary, whole-language represents a shift from the traditional form of reading and language arts instruction that has dominated in American public schools. This approach affords minority students opportunities to interact with literature in a way that allows them to demonstrate their linguistic talents as well as become active, necessary participants in the teaching and learning process.

References

Clark, K. (1994). Whole language and language minority students: A natural fit. (ERIC Document Reproduction Service No. ED 379 946).

Davis, A. (1996). Successful urban classrooms as communities of practice: Writing and identity. (ERIC Document Reproduction. Service No. ED 414 584).

Goodman, K. (1986). What's whole in whole language Portsmouth, NH: Heinemann.

Gross, P., & Shefelbine, J. (1991). Whole language teacher education in multicultural contexts: Living our own models of learning. (ERIC Document Reproduction Service No. ED 359 489).

Hollingsworth, S., Minarik, L., & Teel, K. (1991). Listening for Aaron: A teacher's story about modifying a literature-based approach to literacy to accommodate a young male's voice. East Lansing, MI: National Center for Research on Teacher Learning. (ERIC Document Reproduction Service No. ED 346 082).

Zarillo, J. (1987, August). Literature-centered reading and language minority. Paper presented for the Institute on Literacy and Learning Language Minority Project, University of California.

CHAPTER 3

Mathematics and the Middle School Student

Patsy Williams
Grambling State University Middle Magnet School
Grambling, LA

Now many times have you heard a student gay, "I hate math"? This statement is often made by students in all levels of school, inclusive of college students. Many times students in the lower grades fail to grasp the fundamentals of math. This is to say that many students have not mastered the basic fundamentals of mathematics that will enable them to employ the various concepts displayed in a mathematical situation.

What is mathematics? Mathematics is a phase of science that develops the habits of logical and rigorous thinking which is necessary to pursue specific knowledge that can be applied in one's everyday life. Math requires hard work to be able to understand the "how" and "why" aspect of its components. If you actually take a good look at math, you will see that it only involves four (4) operations: addition, subtraction, multiplication, and division. All other structures of math revolve around these four operations,

As an instructor of middle school math, I have discovered that students who have expresses a "dislike" or "hate" for math must have an experiment with this phase of science that is called "success". Once a student has this "successful" experience, there is a sense of "Mr. or Mrs. Feelgood" within that cannot be withheld. It is then that I notice these once idle and inactive students become more active and involved in the classroom participation. They are now raising their hands, excited, and ready to respond to many mathematical challenges.

In today's classrooms this change of behavior is called motivation. What was implemented within the classroom that has caused this once "hate" of math to "liking" math? Here are some strategies that were instrumental to this change in perception.

Mathematics Notebook

As pan of the requirements for class, students should have a mathematics notebook. This is not a spiral tablet that will be misshaped by the second month of school. This is a three-ringed binder with inside pockets. Within the notebook are five dividers, each bearing one of these headings: Objectives, Definitions, Problem-Solving, Classwork, and Money Matters. Other suggested topics could be Homework, Tests and Quizzes, Extra Practice, etc.

Objectives: In this section, students should record the objectives daily. In addition, students should write and references used including book page(s) and homework if there is not a divider for homework.

Definitions: Students should keep a math vocabulary for future reference. Each vocabulary word should be given on a spelling test with their definition.

Problem-Solving/Critical Thinking. All word problems should be recorded in this section of the notebook. Have students to write the page where each problem came from and the topic of discussion. On some days, place a sensible riddle on the board that will enhance critical thinking.

Classwork: This section should house all the notes that were given in class. This includes examples, scratch work, persona, notes, etc.

Money Matters: This section is used as a bankbook of debits and credits. Students are given play money as rewards for positive behavior, correct responses, homework, or any other behavior. Students have practice in adding and subtracting integers as well as keeping a bankbook that will be useful in the real world. Every Friday, students recite their balance in their amounts. If the students give the correct balance, they are rewarded. If they are incorrect, they are penalized. Students are also penalized for saying "can't", "hard", or any other unacceptable behavior.

Students who have a debit in their account have the opportunity to purchase items that are offered throughout the school year. Some of the items include a pizza party, gift certificates from their store of choice, extra points, hall passes, and ice cream parties. One year there was a year-end "Sales Day" where merchants donated clothes, coupons, food, purses, caps, pizza, and other items that middle school students enjoy, which was sold to them using their own money. This motivational technique has been a big hit!

Poems-Cards-Stories

Often many students have talents that are not used. I have discovered that these talents can be used in a mathematics classroom. I have allowed student to write poems, make cards, and write stories for different occasions. For example, students have had the opportunity to make cards and write stories for Valentine's Day, Thanksgiving, and Christmas. With these cards, students are allowed to draw using their art skills and write using their imaginations to create words that rhyme. It is not expensive to make these items. Construction paper can be used it make the cards by folding a sheet in half. Writings and pictures may be placed on

30

the front, inside, and the back. To write a story, it is required that students use a designated number of numbers and mathematical terms.

Reports

Two major reports are required within the school year. The first is required around October. This report is entitled "How I Will Use Math In My Career". Students are to use a visual aid and no more than two pages of writing to support their idea of a career. Each student gives an oral report and dresses the part of a professional working in their chosen career. This activity gears a middle school student in the direction of a career they might pursue when they become adults.

The second major report is in February for Black History Month. Each student chooses one outstanding Black personality to other information on to write a report. When giving their report, their classmates evaluate them using a rubric. Upon completion of the oral reports, students are placed in cooperative grouping to make up word problems using the information from the written reports in each group. Students are required to make up four (4) problems, each using one of the mathematical operations. This means that each group will have four addition, four subtraction, four multiplication, and four division problems. Afterwards, all of the problems are typed to make up a test to be given to the class.

Mathematics Baseball

This activity is usually played in the classroom with a small group. Divide the class into two teams. The desks are in line against the wall in order to use the center of the room. Bases are made by cutting construction paper in the shape of bases and each base is laminated. A coin is tossed to decide which team will be in home first. Students are given four (4) choices for a hit: single- 10 seconds, double- 15 seconds, triple- 20 seconds, and a home run- 25 seconds. Students are allowed to work the problems on the board while they are timed by the instructor. If a problem is finished on time, whatever choice was made by the student, he/she advances to that position. If the problem is not solved on time, it is counted as an out. Three outs and the teams change position for home team. This activity may be used for many mathematical problems namely; division of decimals, fractions, etc.

Problem Passing

This activity may be used with all operations. Students can be arranged in a circle or arrow. It is recommended not to have more than five in a group. Give a sheet of paper to one student in each group. Give a sheet of paper to one student in each group. The problem is read aloud. The student with the paper has to write the problem and solve it until the word "pass" is said. This procedure continues until all participants have contributed to the problem being solved. This activity may be used for multiplication of mixed numbers, division of fraction, etc.

Write Words for Each Number

This activity helps to enhance spelling skills and is different from the ordinary way of answering a problem. In this activity, have students to write the answers using words rather than writing the numbers.

Journal Writing

Each student has a journal that is written in every Friday. Students are sometimes given a beginning sentence such as "If I Had a Million Dollars, I Would...". On different occasions, students are asked to write the steps to an equation that was given in class during that week.

These are a few of the strategies that have been used to motivate students to experience "success" in my classroom. A student in a mathematics classroom has to remember that learning math is like climbing a ladder. They cannot miss a step.

CHAPTER 4

Critical Barriers To Scientific Literacy

Marilyn M. Irving
Howard University
Washington, DC

Science education has been of great concern in the United States for more than one hundred years. Committees and national level panels have called repeatedly for updating the science curriculum; more "hands-on" approaches; attention to our environment; emphasis on scientific literacy and the processes of science; and other familiar reforms. About every two decades, a reform movement sparks the public interest and promotes changes in the science classroom and in how science is taught.

The present science textbooks and methods of instruction, far from helping, often actually impede progress toward scientific literacy. They emphasize the learning of answers more than the exploration of questions; memory at the expense of critical thought; bits and pieces of information instead of understandings in the context, recitation over argument, reading in lieu of doing. They fail to encourage students to work together; to share ideas and information freely with each other, or to use modem instruments to extend their intellectual capabilities. (Rutherford & Ahlgren, 1990).

Reform documents for science education make a range of recommendations for improving the teaching of science. Among these recommendations are the following: (a) decreasing the information transmission aspects of schooling in favor of increasing attention to the development of authentic scientific and mathematical practices; (b) decreasing the extent of content to the benefit of depth of coverage; (c) changing teachers' roles from orators exposing information to those of intellectual coaches, consultants, or moderators of discussions; and (d) increasing emphasis on reflection n knowledge construction (Brown, Collins, & Duguid 1989; Confrey, 1994). In spite of these recommendations, little change appears to have occurred in science. It has been recognized for almost a century that elementary teachers have inadequate backgrounds in both mathematics and science. Furthermore, and justifiably so, they have little confidence in their ability to successfully teach science. And, as we all know too well, instruction and student learning in science during the elementary grades have left much to be desired for several decades. This is a problem that has consistently vexed those interested in science teacher education.

The National Science Education Standards, Project 2061, and the National Science Teachers Association have all proclaimed that scientific literacy is the most compelling goal of science education. Although there are differences among the various reform documents and for all students and citizens, there is clearly unanimous support for this rather ambitious goal. Few would argue with the laudable goals of scientific literacy. Indeed, it can be argued that the recommendations and visions of the aforementioned learned organizations and reform documents are merely reformulations of educational goals first verbalized nearly a century ago. Although numerous individuals would claim to know the answer, we continue to ask ourselves why so little has changed with respect to the achievement of literacy in science. There are numerous constraints that make change in science instruction especially difficult. Science is extremely abstract in nature. Consequently, instructional time for in-depth understanding in science is extended beyond what may be required in other academic disciplines. Further, the abstract concepts of science require extended time for application, and practice is needed for this discipline to ensure learning that will not quickly deteriorate. Science requires additional time for laboratory activities. These activities often involve expensive equipment and supplies that are unnecessary in other academic disciplines. Finally, the knowledge base of science is continually expanding without any concurrent expansion of allotted time for science instruction.

Traditional objectives for schooling in science have emphasized the transmission of content by means of lectures (Tobin, 1990b; Tobin & Gallagher, 1987). Shocked by the Russian launch of Sputnik, American curriculum reform increasingly focused on laboratory activities as a means for learning science in a more meaningful way. These new curricula were based on the assumption that the structure of nature revealed itself to students as they engaged in hands-on activities leading to the notion of discovery learning (Tamir & Lunetta 1981). In spite of these curricular innovations, students did not appear to develop better understandings. Recent research provides explanations for the failure of these curricula. First, a number of students suggest that the structure of the natural world or the nature of tools cannot be understood apart from the human practices in which they are relevant (Cobb, 1993; Roth, 1995, 1996b). Second, by engaging students in traditional laboratory activities, students appear to learn procedures for following instructions rather than gaining scientific understandings (Amerine & Bilmes, 1990). In recent years, many leading educational theorists have attributed the shortcomings of traditional science teaching to the underlying realist epistemology and have proposed developing new teaching/teaming environments compatible with constructivist and social-constructivist views of knowing and learning (Cobb, Wood, & Yackel, 1991; yon Glasersfeld, 1989; Tobin, 1994). These educational theorists have influenced recent reports and guidelines for the improvement of science education (AAAS, 1989).

Some of the recommendations for change in science teaching have been proposed by educational theorists and reformers. They emphasize the following: (a) sense-making over memorization and indoctrination; (b) student engagement in tool-related and discursive practices over seat work and listening; and (c) a bottom-up approach to teaming that begins with what students know rather than a top-down approach that by and large imposes new frameworks regardless of students' existing common sense (mundane) views of the world. Content coverage has been an important point of contention between more traditional conceptions of science teaching and novel approaches, which are being used today. Traditional approaches focus on "coverage" of a number of concepts specified in official curriculum documents. Approaches informed by constructivist epistemology value understanding over coverage.

This chapter addresses existing discrepancies between current understandings of how scientists and other educators creatively solve problems and contemporary practices of teaching science. Important considerations for redesigning science education are also suggested.

When students do traditional laboratory work, science comes out short: students do learn something, but that often has more to do with turning a set of instructions into an accounted for course of action involving laboratory equipment than it does with actually learning any science (Amerine & Bilmes, 1990; Lynch, Livingston, and Garfinkel, 1983). The cognitive skills tapped and developed by such laboratory tasks are far less theoretical/scientific than practical in nature. A vivid description of current science teaching was provided by ethnographic studies of high school science in Australia and the United States (Gallagher and Tobin 1987; Tobin and Gallagher 1987). These studies identified several problematic elements of laboratory teaching. First, laboratory investigations embody a "cookbook" approach. Students follow recipes, gathering and recording data without a clear sense of the purposes, the procedures, or the interconnections between the two. Second, investigations provide low costive demands that preclude reflective action. Third, students engage in activities not intended by the curriculum planners, spending much of their laboratory time in off-task activity with short periods of attention to complete work. Time off-task is used for non-science-related socialization with peers. Such teaching methods are held responsible for the high numbers of students who drop science in their early high school years. At the same time, those who are not successful learn that science is for a special breed of smart people.

One would expect that with a broader understanding of the nature of science, scientific facts and theories, and scientists' everyday work, public policy-makers would be able to make more informed decisions about priorities for spending public money. Schools are places where such better understandings can be fostered. To bring about change, the social and constructive aspects of everyday practice in science and engineering should be shared with children. Telling children how scientists do science does not necessarily lead to far-reaching changes in how children do science; and it cannot, as long as the school curriculum is based on verbally expressed formal knowledge (Papert, 1991). The geneticist David Suzuki (1989) makes a very explicit link between the quality of science education and being able to function as responsible citizens in an increasingly socio-technical world. He thus suggests changes in science education; we do not need to inculcate children with facts but foster in them an excitement

41

through activities that engage them in exploring, discovering, and connecting.

One design of science learning environments has been based on the assumption that learning occurs through participation in tool-related and discursive practices (Lave, 1993). Thus central to this work were the notions of science as inquiry in ill-structured domains or open inquiry, science as discourse, and cognitive apprenticeship as a learning metaphor.

In an open inquire environment students pursue series of research questions of their own interest. They design experiments and even apparatus and instrumentation to produce data, and through the interpretation of these data, they derive answers to their research questions. In preparing open-inquiry learning environments, five conditions are minimally necessary: (1) participants work and learn in contexts in which some problems are ill-defined; (2) participants experience uncertainties and ambiguities of scientific knowing and learning; (3) learning is driven by the current knowledge state of the participants; (4) participants experience themselves as members of learning communities in which knowledge, practices, and discourses are shared and develop out of members' interactions; and (5) members (apprentices, newcomers) in these communities can draw on the expertise of more knowledgeable others and on any suitable resource that could enhance their learning. Open-inquiry laboratory or design activities can be used for elementary and secondary students, because it's believed that students will develop a new relationship to knowledge: many students no longer consider knowledge as something foreign that they need to acquire just to take the next career step but as something that they construct for themselves, and they see themselves not only as reproducers of cultural knowledge but, more important, as producers of personal knowledge (Lucas & Roth, 1996). However, in most science courses, they still face examinations that focus on factual types of knowledge and they still face undergraduate university courses that focus on factual knowledge and basic skills rather than processes and the applications of technology.

The goal of our instructional changes help students in constructing different images of science and science-related knowledge. New learning environments can bring about changes in students' learning processes, attitudes, learned content, and discourse about the nature of science and scientific knowledge.

Teachers should see themselves as guides and facilitate discussion. When students view learning science as a positive experience they will find it easier to communicate or compare results from science experiences, In addition, they will feel that classes were important learning solve problems on their own. At

43

the same time, students appreciate the presence of teachers to whom they could turn when they felt stuck. Further, students think it is important that they are part of a culture in which collaboration and negotiation are valued.

In summary, traditional science teaching leads to (a) singular and mythical views about science and scientists, (b) scientifically non-literate citizens, and (c) knowledge that is of little use outside schools. In the past six years, studies have been designed and explored on science learning environments that allowed students to develop different understandings and much more critical stances toward science in addition to learning traditionally valued content matter. Learning environments whose design is based on understandings that have emerged from recent science and technology studies (a) lead to student learning and understanding that is qualitatively different from student learning in traditional contexts; (b) create changes in the epistemological commitments of students; and (c) create positive attitudes that are opposite to current trends. Getting students to develop positive attitudes toward science will hopefully increase competence and achievement in science. If science education aspires to the development of a "scientifically literate society," the development of an understanding of scientific practice and competence in science must become core goals.

In conclusion, one of the goals of science educators should be a demand for learning environments in which students learn science through integration of content and pedagogy, and mind/hands-on experiences via using the constructivist model (i.e. allowing students to use their prior knowledge to construct their own knowledge to make sense of science lessons studied).

References

Aikenhead, G. (1992). The integration of STS into science education. *Theory into Practice, 31*:27-35.

American Association for the Advancement of Science (AAAS). (1989). Science for all Americans: Project 2061. Washington, DC: American Association for the Advancement of Science.

Bernstein, B. (1990). The structuring of pedagogic discourse: Class, codes and control. London and New York: Routledge.

Bijker, W. E. (1987). The social construction of Bakelite: Toward a theory of invention. In The social construction of technological systems, edited by W. E. Bijker, T. P. Hughes, and T. J. Pinch, 159-87. Cambridge, MA: MIT Press.

Brookhart, C. V. (1993). School science as a rite of passage: A new frame for familiar problems. Journal of Research in Science Teaching, 30:649-68. V

Brown, J. S.; Collins, A.; & Duguid, P. (1989, January/February). Situated cognition and the culture of learning. *Educational Researcher IS*, 32-42.

Cartsen, W. S. (1993). Teacher knowledge and discourse control: Quantitative evidence from novice teachers' classrooms. *Journal of Research in Science Teaching* 30, 471-81.

Cobb, P., Wood, T., & Yackel, E. (1991). Analogies from the philosophy and sociology of science for understanding classroom life. *Science Education*, 75, 23-44.

Confrey, J. (1994). Learning to see children's mathematics: Crucial challenges in constructivist reform. In The practice of constructivism in science education, edited by K. Tobin, 299-21. Fellsdale, NJ: Lawrence Eribaum.

Fensham, P. J., & Gardner, P. L. (1994). Technology education and science education: A new relationship? In Innovations in science and technology education, edited by D. Layton, 59-70. Paris: UNESCO.

Gallagher, J. J., & Tobin, K. (1987). Teacher management and student engagement in high school science. *Science Education* 71, 535-55.

Garfinkel, H. M. Lynch, M., & Livingston, E. (1981). The work of a discovering science construed with materials from the optically discovered pulsar. *Philosophy of the Social Sciences* (2) 13, 1-58.

Gooding, D. (1992). Putting agency back into experiment. In Science as practice and culture, edited by A. Pickering. 65-112. Chicago: University of Chicago Press.

Latour, B. (1983). Give me a laboratory and I will raise the world. In Science observed: Perspectives on the social study of science, edited by K. D. Knorr-Cetina & M. Mulkay, 141-70. London: Sage.

(1987). Science in action: How to follow scientists and engineers through society. Milton Keynes, UK: Open University Press.

(1992a). Aramis ou I"amour des techniques (Aramis or the love of technology). Paris Editinos la Decoiuverte.

Latour, B., & Fells, S. Woolgar Beverly. CA: Sage.

(1979). Laboratory life: The social construction of scientific facts.

Lave, J. (1988). Cognition in practice: Mathematics and culture in everyday life. Cambridge, LTK: Cambridge University Press.

Lucas, K. B., & Roth, W. M. 1996. The nature of scientific knowledge and student learning: Two longitudinal case studies. *Research in Science Education*, 26, 103-29.

Lynch, M., Livingston, E., & Garfinkel, H. (1983). Temporal order in laboratory work. In Science observed: Perspectives on the social study of science, edited by K.D. Knorr-Cetina and M. Mulkay, 205-38. London: Sage.

McGinn, M. K., Roth, W. M, Boutonne, S., & Woxzczyna, C. (1995). The transformation of individual and collective knowledge in elementary science classrooms that are organized as knowledge-building communities. *Research in Science Education*, 25, 163-89.

Papert, S. (1991). Situating constructionism. In Constructionism: Research reports and essays, 1985-1990, edited by I. Harel and S. Papert, 1-11. Norwood, NJ: Ablex.

Poole, D. 1994. Routine testing practices and the linguistic construction of knowledge. *Curriculum and Instruction*, 12(1),25-50.

Posner, G. J., Strike, K. A., Hewson, P.W., & W. A. Gertzog. (1982). Accommodation of a scientific conception: Toward a theory of conceptual change. *Science Education*, 66(2),11-27.

Roth, W. M. (1994). Experimenting in a constructivist high school physics laboratory. *Journal of Research in Science Teaching* 3(1),197-223.

Roth, W. M., & Bowen, G. M. (1993). An investigation of problem solving in the context of a grade 8 open-inquiry science program. *Journal of the Learning Sciences*, 3, 165-204.

Roth, W. M., & Roychoudhury, A. (1993). The development of science process skills in authentic contexts. *Journal of Research in Science Teaching*, 30(1), 27-52.

CHAPTER 5

Strategies for Strengthening Literacy Learning in a Middle School Science Program

Joyce B. Patton
Caddo Middle Magnet School
Shreveport, LA

Cooperative Learning: A Plus for the Middle School Science Program

Cooperative learning is an attractive instructional format because it enables students to learn from each other (in particular) high ability students can teach lower ability students. It offers an alternative to competitive learning which is disadvantageous to slower students and to students who have become "turned off" to school. David and Roger Johnson state in their book, *Circles of Learning: Cooperation in the Classroom,* cooperative learning environments are superior to competitive or individualistic environments for fostering learning, self-esteem, and positive attitudes toward school and classmates. When I applied cooperative learning in my eighth grade sciences classes, measurable improvements were recognized in my students' understanding of science.

A variety of cooperative learning models have been developed, field tested, and evaluated. Some delineate how tasks are structured and how groups are evaluated. In some models, students work on a single task; in others group members work independently on one aspect of a task, pooling their work when they finish.

Groups may be evaluated in a variety of ways. In some methods the evaluation is based on the sum or average of individual members' performances; in others, the entire group's performance is evaluated. Methods of evaluation range from traditional testing and grading to self-evaluation.

The three methods of cooperative grouping that I employed in my classroom fall into two broad categories: problem solving and tutorial methods. Tutorial methods tend to be structured and teacher-centered, while the problem solving methods are open-ended and student-centered. Both approaches have shown to be effective in helping students learn factual information and become better problem solvers.

Additionally, the incorporation of an alternative assessment method that proved very successful was that of the *scoring rubric*. A scoring rubric consists of a fixed scale and a list of observable criteria that are given a certain numeric value on the scale. Once the objectives are realized a scoring rubric can be developed with the students to define expectations and to assure quality work.

Sample scoring rubric for cooperative group behavior:

O The student does not participate in the cooperative group activity.

1 The student participates as part of the group but does not contribute ideas, does not listen.

2 The student participates as part of the group, contributes ideas, does not listen.

3 The student participates as part of the group, contributes ideas, and listens.

COOPERATIVE LEARNING MODELS

Model I -Laboratory Management: During laboratory periods in my classroom, I used my own version of an approach originated by Lewis and Ostland in their book *Stepping into Successful Science Teaching.* Laboratory Management has five components outlined below.

* *Assign students to lab groups of three.*

* *Within each lab group assign the following roles:*

Group Leader/Organizer: In charge of carrying out the task; asking informational questions of the teacher; picking up and returning materials; in charge of safety; conducting group discussions about processes and results. He/she either conducts the activity or assigns procedures for the activity to other group members.

Reader/Recorder: Responsible for reading aloud all lab procedures to be covered by the group; collects information and records it at the computer or on worksheets, tables or graphs; certifies the results that are recorded as being the consensus of the whole group.

Checker: Responsible for asking questions to make sure all members of the group understand the materials and making sure that all members of the group participate.

* Introduce the investigation or pre-lab.
* Have the students conduct their investigation with each group
  member performing his/her assigned roles.
* Discuss the results of the investigation with the group.
* Clean up.

A group laboratory report may be turned in instead of a report from each student. Before the report is turned in, each group member should review the report before signing the report as being acceptable by him/her. Each of the group members will receive the same grade for the laboratory report. The same laboratory group may be maintained for a grading period. However, the roles should be rotated among the group members so that within the grading period each student will have to assume each of the three roles.

Sample rubric for scoring laboratory report:

O The experiment is not set up or carried out.

1 The experiment is set up sloppy; some procedures are followed; the results are inaccurate; Clean up is done.

2 The experiment is set up correctly; some procedures are followed; the results are inaccurate. Clean up is done.

3 The experiment is set up correctly; procedures are followed correctly some results are accurate. Clean up is done.

4 The experiment is set up correctly; procedures are followed correctly; results are accurate. Clean up is done.

In quizzes over the laboratory work, each group member will receive a bonus if all members of the group scores 80% or better on the quiz.

Model II: STAD

STAD (Student Team Achievement Division) was originated by Robert Slavin and his colleagues at John Hopkins University in 1986. ST AD can be easily implemented into the traditional, textbook curriculum. Therefore, if you are interested in using cooperative learning in your classroom, STAD is an excellent model with which to begin. STAD had four components outlined below.

*Teach -The teacher presents the materials, concepts, skills, and processes that the students are to learn. The presentation can be a lecture, lecture/demonstration, computer simulation, multimedia presentation.

*Study in Teams -Teams are composed of four or five students who represents a balance in terms of academic ability, gender, and ethnicity. After the teams are organized, students complete approximately one lesson together, working with prepared study materials such as computer simulations, worksheets and workbook activity pages or sets of questions based on the unit of study. Inform students that the activities are designed to help them help each other prepare for a quiz. Each team of students works together to answer questions. They can work in pairs within each team, and then to encourage team members to take responsibility for all of the work:

1) make sure that each member can answer each question correctly.

2) have students answer questions on their own as often as possible.

3) insist that team members explain their answers to questions.

*Test individually -After the work is completed, administer a quiz to measure knowledge students have gained. Students are not permitted to help each other.

*Improvement Scores -Assign an "individual improvement score" to encourage students to work harder. Establish a base score -the the minimum score on the quiz -for each student. Individual base scores are determined by the teacher, based on each student's previous performance. Several students may be identified each week, representing as many team members as possible. Improvement in learning is as important as the scores.

Model III Jigsaw II

Jigsaw II was developed by Eliot Aronson in 1978. It is a cooperative learning model in which students become experts on a part of the instructional material about which they are learning. The expert groups are groups of team members studying the same topic. By becoming an expert, and then teaching other members of their team, students become responsible for their own learning. The Jigsaw II model has the advantage of encouraging students of all abilities to be responsible to the same degree, although the depth and quality of their reports will vary .

Jigsaw II is also an excellent model to incorporate the use of the computer along with a multimedia program such as

HyperStudio. Students learn content-area curriculum as well as computer skills. Four important elements of Jigsaw II are outlined below:

Expose all students to the same material.

Preparation of materials -Develop an expert sheet and a quiz for each unit of study. The expert sheet should communicate what students should do, such as read, watch a video or multimedia presentation, or do an activity, and it should also contain an outline of the topic in the form of questions. Each student in a team should be responsible for a different part or focus.

Teams and expert groups -Students are assigned the same topic representing different teams and meet together in an expert team to review and study the topic. For example in a study of the Ocean, one team of experts would concentrate on properties of ocean water while another team may examine ocean floor topography and a third team could explore the ocean life zone. Distribute the expert sheets among each expert team. Give students time to work on their topic prior to meeting in their expert groups.

Your expert sheet will be important, as they direct the students to activities, materials, and questions. Encourage diversity in learning methods. Groups might do hands-on activities, read from reference books, or use a computer for simulation. The group's goal is to learn about the subtopic and to prepare a brief presentation that group members will use to teach the material to members of their respective learning teams.

This would be an excellent time to design a HyperStudio project for each group to construct a stack to present information to their peers. As they work through the project, students would learn both content and enhance computer objectives (e.g. terminology: stacks, buttons, text box, graphic, navigate, scroll etc. Skills: creating multimedia storyboards, text and graphic boxes, buttons and adding transitions). They would apply the skills by researching using electronic encyclopedias and the Internet as well as traditional methods.

Reports and quizzes -Students return to their home team and teach their information to the learning team. Encourage students to use a variety of teaching methods. They can demonstrate the idea, read a report, use the computer, or illustrate their ideas with photographs or diagrams. Encourage team members to discuss the reports and ask questions, as each team member is responsible for learning about all the subtopics.

After expert teams are finished reporting, conduct a brief class discussion or a question and answer session. Then administer a quiz to each individual, using the same process of scoring and reporting described in STAD. As group members learn to nurture and support on another, they also begin to develop respect across the boundaries of race, ethnicity, and social class.

Summary

In a cooperative group, students may develop higher levels of trust, feel less vulnerable to taking risks, and feel more comfortable than in the class as a whole. Intrinsic motives such as interest, curiosity, and desire for understanding often arise in group exploration. Students often develop a sense of competence in their own abilities to reason and solve problems.

Teachers foster positive interdependence among students in cooperative grouping by helping them to divide work loads, decide upon a goal, and differentiate roles. Physical arrangement of the classroom so that students can sit and talk in small groups is a must.

Presenting a scoring rubric gives students a criteria for success. It defines what is expected and how they will be graded. Teachers must hold each individual in a group accountable for the material covered, and see that each student contribute to the achievement of the group's goal. Cooperative learning affords three key concepts to student team learning: team rewards, individual accountability , and equal opportunities for success. At the same time it affords the teacher the opportunity to release some of his/her control over the learning situation and share the responsibility with students, releasing dramatic potential for creativity.

References

Aronson, E. (1978). *The Jigsaw Classroom.* Beverly Hills, CA: SAGE Publications.

Lewis, M., & Ostlund, K. L. (1985). *Stepping into Successful Science Teaching.* San Marcos, TX: Edwards Aquifer Research and Data Center.

Johnson, D. W., & Johnson, R. T. (1993). *Circles of Learning Cooperation in the Classroom,* Alexandria, VA: Association for Supervision and Curriculum Development.

Slavin, R. (1985). *Using Student Team Learning.* Baltimore, MD: The John Hopkins Team Learning Project.

HyperStudio, http://hyperstudio.6.

CHAPTER 6

Writing a Book of Their Own: A Key to Literacy Development

Nancy Shepard,
Poet, Author, Teacher
Lake Charles, LA

As an educator seeking to eradicate illiteracy, I found a marvelous means: having students write and publish their own books. According to the literature on reading and motivation, students increase engaged time and retain and apply more knowledge when learning activities are active and relevant to their lives

In this chapter I share the rationale for and strategy of student-produced books, which I used to enhance my students' literacy skin development.

Writing a Book: The Key to Literacy

How-to write a book and get it published as a literacy skill across the curriculum is most timely and most appropriate as educators seek means of eradicating illiteracy. As a health educator, I found about 20% of my students lacked skills writing research papers or simply being able to read the printed work. As sad and dismal as the situation was, I knew too as a creative writer that it was important for students to be able to read well and quickly. I also knew if they were to master the course, every student must, without undue delay, be able to read the contents of the textbook or other material that form a part of this course. The good students were efficient readers. They read rapidly with good comprehension and retained what they read. For the slow reader, this was not so. They seemed to read at a slower pace, when and if they could pronounce the words.

Reading is the key to obtaining a successful education. If a student can't read, he can't write. If he can't write, he can't pass his courses, which will make him unable to obtain a quality education and graduate. If he can't graduate, he can't get any type of decent employment and he will more likely become an unhappy individual and failure in life.

Being dissatisfied to say the least with the lack of writing and communicating skills of my students, I asked the principal to allow me to teach a course in reading and writing skills in the upcoming semester. The principal granted my wish.

My first approach to reach the students and sweep them along with me, was to state the purpose of the class, which was to teach reading and writing and to make it so much fun that the students would eventually write their own book and have it published. I asked some of the students to read aloud for me. This act was to explore their reading level, which I found to be average and above to my surprise. With this newfound information, I presented the plight of the class and where we would begin and hopefully, where we would end. The end was at the publishing company, of course.

Previewing was first on the agenda. A good way for a reader to approach a new course or text is to devote a few minutes to previewing the material. This is a useful reading technique by which the reader familiarizes himself with the contents of the text before he begins the actual reading. A few tips given were:

1. Read the titles and subtitles. If the titles have been well prepared, they will indicate the main ideas of the material. The subtitles generally indicate the various points that go logically under the main idea.

2. Examine the diagrams, charts and other visual aids.

3. Pay attention to the length of paragraphs, and let them determine the speed at which to read the selection. Long paragraphs are apt to mean more detailed texts: short one give fewer details and constitute easier texts. Read the long ones more slowly, the short ones more quickly.

The class consisted of students of various nationalities. Its duration was six months, five days a week. Students met the following objectives:

1. They learned the proper and correct use of grammar. Definition: Grammar describes the way a language works; the study of words in sentences. English Grammar tells how English works in communicating ideas. Ideas are generally expressed in sentences.

A.   Sentence

B.   Sentence fragments –

C.   Comma splice

D.   Verb form

E.   Mechanics

    1. Manuscripts

    2. Capitals

    3. 3. Italics

    4. Abbreviations

F.   Punctuation

    1. The comma

    2. Superfluous comma

    3. Semicolon

    4. The apostrophe

    5. Quotation marks

G. The period

H. Spelling and diction

I. Effective sentences

J. The paragraph

K. The book

II. They were taught the following steps on "How to write a book and get it published":

A. Tools Needed:

    1. Writing pens

    2. Proper paper

    3. Erasers

    4. Writer's Market directory

    5. Journals

    6. Computers

F. Structure of a book

C. Book format

D. Book content

E. Book illustrations

F. Grant directory

G. Importance of copyrights

H. Importance of ISBN numbers

I. Manuscript

J. Query letters

    Once the reading and writing levels of the students progressed, they were introduced to the skills of writing their own book. This act seemed appeal to their need to excel and achieve.

Names of writers and published authors were presented to them in different and many ways. Published authors visited the class. Some of the students had never met any writers knew any for that matter.

When Maya Angelou visited our fair city, some of the students were allowed to meet her at the reception and concert. After Ms. Angelou's visit, all wanted to write poetry and become a famous writer: I was elated with their newfound courage and self-confidence. I then introduced them to the production of writing their book and the tools they needed and must acquire and master. Production came last and the following was taught:

A self-publisher is one who directly contracts with a book manufacturer and their production department. The writer owns the rights and only pays for services that are needed to get the book into print. He has complete control of every aspect of the work.

There are three major divisions in the field of publishing: 1) Traditional, 2) Vanity/Subsidy, and 3) Self-publishing. The *traditional publisher* is one that contracts with a writer for a book and *incurs* all costs in the production and advertising, and pays the writer a royalty on the books sold. The writer has little or nothing to say about the book or its production. The *vanity or subsidy publishers* are those who promise to produce the book while sharing in the cost. They have a negative reputation in the Trade because the author pays for all the costs in production and marketing, yet the publisher owns the work, You can always tell a vanity press, because they will contact you once you copyright your work, Avoid them at all costs. The *self publisher is* one who directly contracts with a book manufacturer to be their production department He owns all the rights and only pays for what services are needed to get the book into print. He will have complete control of every aspect of the work.

If one chooses to self-publish his work he will need to follow the guidelines listed below:

MANUSCRIPT

After the story is complete, have it professionally edited. Romance Writers of America, a non-profit professional/educational association of 8,200 romance writers and other industry professionals, provide editorial as well as critiquing services for a small fee. Before submitting the manuscript to an editor, make sure it is double spaced and has an extra wide right hand margin, about three to four inches, The editor will use the wide margin to make corrections and notes.

FORMATTING

After the manuscript has been edited, it will need to be formatted on disk. There are thousands of different typefaces but always use Times Roman. It is the easiest to read. Changing typeface should be one of the first tasks. This task should also include headers and/or footers for title, author name, and page number. Spacing should be changed from double to single. Margins or line lengths should be changed to reflect the size of the book.

COPYEDITING

Once the book has been formatted, it needs to be gone reviewed, page by page, to make sure the chapter headings begin on the same line for each chapter. Also check for the following giveaways that the book has not been professionally typeset:

* Dashes made with two hyphens instead of an *"em"* dash (a dash the length of the letter m),

* Two spaces after a mark of punctuation instead of one space,

* Underlining words instead of using italics.

* Inch marks (also called tick marks) used instead of book or closed quotations.

* The last word on a page hyphenated,

*   A single word or a one-line end of a sentence dangling by itself at the top or bottom of a page, which is called either a widow and/or orphan.

After the book has been edited, formatted and copyedited, the pages can be printed out for the book manufacturer.

DESIGN OF COVER

The cover is what captures the attention of customers. If he is going to put money anywhere in the book's production, it should be in the design and color of the cover. The cover is the one part of the book, which should be produced professionally. Unless an artist, or designer, or photographer by profession is hired to design the cover, it will be difficult to come up with a design that will be marketable.

Check local art schools for graduates who have built a career in commercial art, or interview commercial artists or illustrators from an artist's guild such as the San Francisco Society of Illustrators, 690 Market Street, San Francisco, California.

WORKING WITH A BOOK MANUFACTURER

After the cover has been designed and the manuscript has been edited, formatted, copyedited, and printed out, the next step is to submit the manuscript to a book manufacturer. He may want to select a book manufacturer before beginning any of the above because some may handle the formatting. Please note that there is a big difference between a printer and a book manufacturer. The latter specializes in printing books.

Know how you want book design to look. That is the key to working well with book manufacturers. Do not be embarrassed to ask questions. A book is ready to be made into camera-ready pages after it has been designed, typeset, and proofread.

MARKETING PLAN

Publication Date: (Fall Season Release)

Distribution: Major Distributor/Wholesales, Trade Shows and
Conventions

Concept: Historical Fiction

Target Audience: Readers of historical romance

Target Markets: Gift Shops, Mailing List, Newsletters—Ethnic,
Oriental, Mail Order Catalogs, Book Clubs, Chain and
Independent Book Stores

Overall Strategies,

 * Use Black print and broadcast media to increase public
awareness of the book,

 * Set up book event tour at independent bookstores. These

events will be designed to quickly inform readers of book. Q&A to follow.

* Advertise directly to consumers and bookstores through mailing list.

* Submit articles to magazines and newsletters on the topic of Black History and romance novels.

* Investigate co-op trade shows exhibiting opportunities for book fairs and expos.

* Submit title for book awards.

Advance Review Media

Romantic Times

Small Press

Targeted Media (specific breakdowns forthcoming)

Editors of major urban newspapers

Daytime TV and Cable community talk shows

Promotional Strategies & Special Events

* Book release events through African American Bookstores

* Fundraisers for Black History programs

* Ten city book event and promotions tour

* "En Advance" Newsletter/Catalog to be used as a promotional tool

* Explore foreign rights sales possibilities

*   Submit book for awards and honors

REVIEW COPIES

A review copy is the final draft of the manuscript, bound with a plastic comb on the spine. The cover is usually index card stock printed with the book and contact information. It is the complete book with the following information: author's name, price, book dimensions, subject matter, distribution channels and format. A brief synopsis of the book is located on the inside cover. Send it to reviewers, distributors and wholesalers, mail order catalogs and book clubs, Send this out three six months in advance of the publication date.

MARKETING

One may think that after the manuscript has been edited and proofed, and the book has been sent to the book manufacturer that it is time to pop open the champagne and celebrate, NOT. Marketing a book takes a lot of time and resources and one may very well spend more time marketing the book than writing it!

Develop marketing tools once the manuscript is complete. There are two basic types of marketing tool- sales tools and promotional tools. A *sales tool* is designed to elicit a sale or demonstrate sales potential. A *promotional tool* is designed to gain media exposure or otherwise bring information about the book to the attention of the public

BOOK RELEASE

The most useful marketing tool is the book release. One is included with a flat cover of the book or a postcard with the book cover printed on the front to all contacts. A book release in the kits should be sent to sales or media contacts, such as bookstores, newspapers, and magazines. It should be no longer than one page.

MARKETING PLAN

It is necessary to set up distribution channels, find markets for the title, and effectively promote the title to target audiences. These goals must be met in order to achieve success, and if any one is neglected, the book will not sell. In order to accomplish these goals, and accomplish them in order, it is necessary to first devise a *marketing, plan.* Without a clear marketing plan, it is going to be difficult trying to sell books, no matter how good the book is. The marketing plan must:

1.   Identify target audience.

2.   Identify retail markets that are most likely to carry the title.

3.	Provide a method of distribution will make the title available for consumers.

4.	Promote the title to the largest segment of the target audience.

5.	Provide a time frame that ensures these steps occur in sequence.

6.	Develop marketing and promotional tools to help reach the above goals.

Before developing marketing plan, ask yourself the following questions. Who is my target audience? Where do I find this audience? Why do they want or need this book? When should I begin each phase of marketing plan so that it moves smoothly?

Pricing

Setting the price of the book can be simple or complicated, whichever one chooses. For the sake of simplicity, the price is usually five time the cost of the book that is, if the cost is $2 to manufacture the book, then 5 x $2 = $10. The book should be priced at $10. Note: the cost should include, editing, printing, and postage (for review copies).

A while ago, I taught a creative writing class to a group of students with limited literacy skills and problems with low self-esteem. The students were taught creative writing, and how it can be divided into fiction, faction, and non-fiction. Fiction is invented. Non-fiction is based on facts. Factions consist of both fictions and non-fiction. Writers choose one or several forms in which to do their work. Novels, short stories, drama, poems, essays, and biographies are a few examples a writer can use to express his work.

During class time, the students worked on projects that included different writing styles: short stories, novels or collections of poems were used. They discussed their work with me and each other, frequently reading parts aloud. Through their actual writing and receiving constructive criticism, they learned something about plotting, character, description, writing dialogue and other aspects of writing.

Students were encouraged to submit their manuscripts to publishing companies and log an accurate account of acceptances and rejections.

The establishment of this class allowed me to work with students who had below average and average literacy skills and low self-esteem. These students rose above their illiteracy and environment and achieved gratification and satisfaction in becoming successful writers. Five students in the class went on to have their books published and are now published authors.

Somewhere in the mix of the class, the students and I both met our objectives. My book, *"99 Pounds"*, was published. For some students, digging for the gold was worth more than the prize. They were not able to have their books published, but they did strengthen their muscles.

CHAPTER 7

Involving Children with Children's Literature:
Strategies That Work

Ellen Butler
Grambling State University
Grambling, LA

"I don't like to read." "I don't want to read." "I can't read that!" How many times have you heard students make remarks similar to these? Probably too many times.

The easy thing for us to do is to ignore students such as those with these attitudes and focus our energy on teaching those who want to read and want to learn. But a characteristic of a "true" teacher is that we do not ignore anyone. We accept the challenge of finding those "tried and true" methods of teaching that can change a student's mind about how they don't like to read or don't want to read. Oh, yes, we have to compete with television, video games and other sorts of high-tech games and entertainment, which is not an easy task. It would be easy to forget about helping those with difficulties. A "good" teacher usually doesn't take the "easy" route and surely doesn't give up.

Throughout the next few pages I want to share some methods that I, as a classroom teacher and librarian, have used to help students develop a love for reading.

READ TO CHILDREN

Many children come to school without having had anyone read to them. Reading to children from the time of conception can make a difference. Softly reading a book calms the child so that s/he will sit and listen to a book and eventually sit and learn in class. Children who are exposed to books at an early age usually like books and are anxious to learn to read them. They begin by reading the pictures and then by reading the words. Being able to touch and hold a book lets the child become a friend of the book.

TEACH CHILDREN VOCABULARY

Talking with children helps to develop their vocabulary. After they have developed a speaking vocabulary, gradually introduce them to written language. Using flashcards, reading words on their favorite cereal box, or words on their toys is a good way to be in. Not all students learn vocabulary in the same way. There are many ways to teach vocabulary. A few examples are:

1. Flashcards-Put one word on each flashcards Begin with a few (about ten) for the first week. Add five new vocabulary cards

each week afterwards.

2. Picture Clues-Put a picture and the word for that picture on a page and make a booklet of the pages. (Have a picture of a dog and the word dog on a page. On another page put a picture of a bird and the word bird.) The child learns to read the words by associating them with the picture.

3. Sentences- Underneath a picture, write one sentence using familiar vocabulary. The child now will learn to read the vocabulary from left to right as a sentence to tell about the picture. Later have two sentences underneath the picture. Soon the child will be able to read paragraphs.

I recall a student who, in third grade, had just begun to read the very simplest words. Each week he was given five words on flashcards, which he carried like a wallet in his pocket. He became very excited when he could pull them out and read them to someone. By the end of that year, he had begun to read a book on beginning second grade level. He would beg for someone to stop and listen to him read his book. He was so proud of himself and he wanted everyone to know he had learned to read. He will continue to need some extra help to catch up, but how wonderful it feels to know he can read.

PEER TUTORING

Students like to play teacher and school. Pair students in a "buddy" system and let them help each other with vocabulary flashcards or take turns reading to each other. In our fast paced society, parents say they are too busy and don't have time to help their children. What a blessing they are missing! One of the greatest joys a parent can have is helping their child to become successful.

ROLE PLAYING

Some stories are perfect for role-playing by children. Let each choose a character and role-play or act out the story they have read. This is one of the best methods for improving comprehension. They retell the story recalling main events, sequence of events, and details. As they retell the story, they also demonstrate an understanding of the character's emotions and express the different moods of the characters.

A different angle for role-playing is for you to tell the story and let the students participate by giving sound effects, at the appropriate time, or by acting out the parts as you tell the story.

PUPPETS

As students enter the library, I have a puppet on my hand. As I read or tell the story using the puppet, the students are spellbound. It doesn't matter whether they are Pre-K or sixth graders, students enjoy puppetry. As I tell the story of <u>Armadillo Rodeo</u> by Jan Brett the students learn how the armadillo rolls up, how they have poor eyesight and how they move on such short legs. The younger students enjoy the Clifford puppet, Corduroy, or Curious George. When they see the puppet, they get very excited and eagerly await the story.

ACCELERATED READER

The latest program that I have added to our library/media center is the Accelerated Reader Program. Books with test software have been purchased. Each book that has a computerized test is marked with a dot on the spine. Inside the front cover is a label showing the title, author, test number, reading level, and points to be earned on the test. Students check out the books, read them, and return to take the computerized test. Upon completion of the test, their score and points earned are shown on the screen. At the end of the year, local businesses of our town donate items to be given to the students as a reward for the number of points earned. The more points a student have, the bigger the prizes.

Needless to say, the students work very hard to earn all the points the can. In the last one and one-half years, since the program has been implemented, the students' reading levels have improved by a year or two. The reading scores on standardized tests have improved. The students are actually reading the books they are checking out. At the end of the year, I hear them say things like, "I can't wait until next year!" or "I am going to get the most points next year!". During this past year, I had some students to read, take tests, and accumulate points on two to seven books a week. They are excited about reading.

It is a good feeling when a student complains if something happened and they didn't get to come to the library or when a student begs you to make time, even is you have a full schedule, to help him.

My reward comes with the student who becomes so excited when s/he has made 100% on their computerized test. They grin from ear to ear, and walk on air to get to the room to share the good news.

The enthusiasm shown by the classroom teacher is an important part of this program. If the student knows the teacher cares and is excited about how many books they've read and how many points they've earned, they will be motivated to work harder. Enthusiasm and excitement are contagious.

These are only a few strategies that I have used successfully in my classroom and library. There are many others that may be just as successful. Whatever the method, the key to remember is that all children can learn. What works for one may or may not work for another. The ultimate measurement of a strategy is, "Did the students learn to read?"

FLANNEL OR MAGNETIC BOARD STORIES

Make flannel board or magnetic board cutouts to use as you tell a story. As you manipulate the different pieces, you are able to capture the students' interests.

Another idea is to let the students place the characters on the board as you tell story. This keeps them actively involved, which allows for greater learning. Any manipulative that students can use keeps them actively involved and enhances their learning.

BOOKS OR BOOKLETS

Developing a student's writing skills is very important. Connecting the writing and reading skills is an interesting and exciting challenge. Begin in first grade by letting students write a sentence or two about a picture. After a few weeks of practice with this idea, broaden their skills by letting them draw a picture and write sentences to tell about it. As their skills progress, develop small books that they can write and illustrate.

Here are a few examples:

Connect paper plates with brads and make a caterpillar. On each plate write a sentence for the story.

A book shaped like an umbrella will be perfect to write a story about "What I Do When It Rains" or a book shaped like a dog holding a bone is best for a story about "My Dog".

CHARACTERIZATION

When telling stories and introducing students to books in our library, I portray the characters by dressing in the costume of that character. For Pre-K and Kindergarten, I dress up like Mother Goose as I introduce the rhymes.

First graders enjoy the story of "Little Red Riding Hood" as I wear a red cape with a hood and carry a filled basket of food and tell the story.

Second and third graders get to meet *Amelia Bedelia*. As I tell different situations of the stories, I am dressed as *Amelia Bedelia* and have different props for the stories. (I put a pair of yellow overalls on the chicken as I "get it dressed"; show a box of dusting powder as I "dust the furniture", etc.) At the conclusion of my presentation, students always want to check out the books about *Amelia Bedelia* written by Peggy Parish. This is only one example of books that can be presented in this way. There are numbers of others that can be introduced by dressing up and portraying the characters.

CHAPTER 8

The Three "R's" of Critical Literacy:
Roots, Reading and Reconstruction

Nanthalia W. McJamerson, Ph. D.
A. Kadir Nur-Hussen, Ph. D.
Jewel Jackson, Ph. D.
Teacher Education Department
Grambling State University
Grambling, LA

Mary Scott Hobdy, M. A.
Executive Assistant to the President, Retired
Grambling State University
Grambling, LA

Literacy skills which empower students result from more than a basic literacy campaign. Critical pedagogy is necessary to prepare students to be their own agents for social change, their own creators of democratic culture (Giroux, 1997, Shor, 1980, 1992). This chapter is based on an inquiry into what happened when an approach to teaching for critical thinking was implemented as an integral part of an aesthetic education curriculum (Washington-McJamerson, 1987) and revisited a decade later (McJamerson, 1998). The researchers investigated ways by which teaching behavior empowers or cripples students with respect to critical thinking--questioning and transforming their social world. In an effort to understand critical teaching, the case study examined two teachers' attempts to implement the critical thinking pedagogy that was embodied in a two-year aesthetic education project. Using observation and interview data, the researcher compared the teachers' patterns of behavior and the influences upon those patterns in relation to (1) opportunities for student control, (2) revelation of the roots of school content, and (3) the connection of school knowledge to personal life (Washington-McJamerson, 1987).

The Berlak and Berlak (1981) Dilemma Language of Schooling was used to clarify the variation in the behavior and influences upon behavior of the teachers. The dilemma language, arranged in three sets--control, societal and curricular--depicts the schooling act as a reflexive process involving tensions toward opposing poles. The Dilemma Language provides a fuller understanding of ways by which teachers' behaviors solicit, instruct or stifle critical thinking and shows ways in which teachers' social experiences influence those schooling acts.

Findings from the study show that both teachers displayed some behavior, which operated in favor of teaching for critical thinking while their behavior, at other times, stifled or presented barriers to teaching for critical thinking. The use of the Berlak and Berlak dilemma language allowed a unique view of the "combination of opposites" in teachers' actions and a view of the influences upon their actions, revealing that there are both problems and possibilities for teaching approaches which can develop the will and capacity to think critically.

Both teachers noted positive implementation influences in the school setting, those conducive for the critical thinking approach, including the encouragement by the principal, project training workshops and materials, as well as the children's academic and social growth and the children's enjoyment of aesthetic education schooling experiences.

The positive factors, however, were confronted by forces which opposed teaching for critical thinking. First, the teachers' social experiences influenced them. Both Mrs. Richards and Mrs. Fairburn recalled that they had been exposed to teacher-controlled schooling experiences as students, as examples of the way school is "supposed" to be. Furthermore, their teacher training and subsequent teaching experience focused upon the textbook, not upon the students' concerns. Thirdly, there were several negative influences in the school context. The Iman School District emphasized high test scores, not critical thinking. The educational trend was "back to basics" rather than "beyond the basics." Resistance, therefore, arose to the use of "basics" time for additional curriculum content. Also, in the school context, the district administration did not support the new curriculum with either facilities or personnel. Some of the time and energy that might have been used for developing critical literacy through aesthetic education was usurped for public relations and positive visibility for the school. This was evident when teachers marveled at the aesthetic, social, academic, and creative growth of their students and, yet, their primary concern was whether the effects of aesthetic education would show in students' scores on the California Achievement Test.

In summary, the "3 Rs" of teaching for critical thinking were (1) student control, (2) revelation of the roots of school knowledge and (3) the connection of school learning to real life. The opposition was the "3 Rs" of tradition and trend were (1) rules, (2) rituals, and right-answer giving (Washington-McJamerson, 1987). Teaching for critical thinking, in the form of aesthetic education, advocated a high degree of student control whereas traditional wisdom advocated teacher control. Teaching for critical thinking sought to reveal the nature of knowledge and of its producers, in order to demystify and empower students while such efforts and concerns were absent from traditional school. Rather, traditional emphasis was upon mastering selected, legitimated school content. Finally, teaching for critical thinking had as its goal students' ownership and use of knowledge for the purpose of making a difference in enhancing their lives, whereas conventional wisdom advocated mastery of content for the purpose of succeeding in society via performing well on standardized tests and obeying the rules.

Recommendations For Curriculum Developers and Teacher Education Programs.

The study showed that it is not opulence of the training atmosphere, the quality of curriculum materials, time allocation, nor mandates that result in implementation of a critical teaching approach. Rather, several other factors are crucial. First, teacher educators must consider what is "in the heads" of teachers whom they train. Teachers' assumptions exerted powerful "pulls" both for and against critical teaching. Secondly, in the process of teacher training, trainers must allow teachers to use their own "voices." Teachers bring knowledge, experience, goals, and views of school and life success to the training setting. Those should be solicited and negotiated or utilized.

The findings of the study also suggest that exposure to a particular teaching approach is not sufficient for its implementation. Teachers must be taught all aspects (theoretical framework, assumptions, form, and content) of the particular craft. This is especially important when learning the craft of teaching for critical thinking, as it is different from, and in some ways the opposite of, conventional and traditional teaching approaches.

The full context of the schooling process should be considered in the training activity, as teaching is not an isolated process but rather a part of a complex socialization network. Political priorities (such as public relations, desegregation, test score mentality) were manifest in the school activity, in the district office and at the societal level and thus exercised powerful influence within and upon teachers. Such forces cannot be ignored in a serious effort to implement critical teaching.

93

Recommendations For Further Research.

This study represented only a small chasm in the revelation of interconnections of teaching behavior, conscious and context as they related to teaching for critical thinking. It illuminated the fact that teaching for critical thinking is up against a powerful network of opposing forces. Much more of the subtlety and complexity of that network needs to be clarified.

Recommendations For Teachers and Community Leaders.

The Berlaks' dilemma framework used in the study showed the tensions between teaching for critical thinking and conventional teaching. The dilemmas revealed that conflicting tendencies not only existed in the classroom but also in the school setting, in the community and at the societal level. That is, the components of teaching for critical literacy opposed some of our cherished traditions and popular trends. The insights about opposition to critical teaching can be used by teachers, parents and community leaders to counteract, negate or prevent barriers to critical literacy.

Teaching for critical thinking involves struggle. The struggle continues. This study offered insights about both the problems and possibilities for developing empowered critical thinkers.

References

Berlak, A. and Berlak, H. (1981). The Dilemmas of Schooling. London: Methuen.

Beyer, L.E. (1979). Schools, Aesthetic Forms, and Social Reproduction. Madison: University of Wisconsin.

Giroux, Henry A. (1997). Pedagogy and the Politics of Hope: Theory, Culture, and Schooling. Boulder, CO: Westview Press.

Giroux, H. A. (1978). Writing and Critical Thinking in the Social Studies. Curriculum Inquiry, 8(1), 291-310.

Hale, J. (1994). Unbank the Fire: Visions for the Education of African American Children. Baltimore: The Johns Hopkins University Press.

McJamerson, N. (1998). "'Immunity to the 'Immaculate' Perception". In G. Duhon-Boudreaux (Ed.), An Interdisciplinary Approach to Issues and Practices in Teacher Education. New York: Edwin Mellen Press.

Shor, I. (1992). Empowering Education: Critical Teaching for Social Change. Chicago: University of Chicago Press.

Wolin, S. J. and Wolin, S. (1993). The Resilient Self. How Survivors of Troubled Families Rise Above Adversity. New York: Villard Books.

CHAPTER 9

Community Coordinating Council, Inc.: A Community-Based Effort Which Supports the Literacy Development Efforts of the School

Valena P. Lane
Community Coordinating Council, Inc.
Grambling, LA

Community Coordinating Council, Incorporated, a non-profit organization providing educational and cultural enrichment experiences for youth and senior citizens, was organized in July, 1997. The goal is to become one of Louisiana's premiere service-oriented organizations helping to improve the quality of life for citizens in a four-parish area- Bienville, Claiborne, Lincoln and Union. Twelve towns/cities, namely, Arcadia, Athens, Bernice, Gibsland, Grambling, Haynesville, Homer, Junction City, Lisbon, Ruston, Simsboro and Summerfield and more than one thousand residents have been touched during the past thirty months of operation. We believe that no other local organization matches us in terms of geographical coverage and diverse offerings of educational seminars, workshops, academies and travel. A five-member board of directors, who presently serve a term of two years, governs the organization.

Our agency knows that a community can be transformed when all the available resources collaborate to make a positive difference. An enormous amount of time and effort is spent coordinating and planning various experiences, which support the literacy efforts of the school. The various programmatic thrusts of this organization will be described in this chapter.

YOUTH LEGISLATURE PROGRAM

Annually, students in grades nine through twelve participate in a series of workshops designed to give them first-hand experiences in writing, presenting and lobbying bills to be debated at the annual Youth Legislative Conference in Baton Rouge, La. The agency invites professors from the Political Science Department of Grambling State University to serve as workshop presenters helping students to become acquainted with the legislative process and preparing them for the conference. At the conference, the participants experience the entire legislative process using the same facilities that their senators and representatives used. It is quite rewarding to hear them debate issues of importance through this mock legislative process.

EDUCATIONAL SEMINARS

In the first twenty-four months, a portion of the programmatic thrust focused on seminars designed to address issues and concerns relative to youth. The participants were transported to one of the twelve towns to hear outstanding speakers and drama presentations. Some of the topics were:

Drug Awareness

Career Counseling (BE ALL YOU CAN BE)

Test Taking Strategies

Triple AAA - Alternative Actions to Anger

Emergent Literacy: Building Strong Foundations for Reading

How to Walk the Tight Rope of Life without Failing Off

Making Responsible Choices

We Care

Get Real- Don't Get Pregnant

Communicating With Victims of Alzheimer's Disease

This activity gave the participants the opportunity to mingle and make friends with children from other parishes while achieving the goals of the programs. There were many friendships established and the collaborative volunteer efforts of the business firms, schools, churches and civic organizations helped all of us to make a positive difference in the fives of the participants.

CULTURAL ENRICHMENT

The greatest satisfaction from our cultural enrichment program came from hearing the phrases cited below by our participants:

"IF IT HAD NOT BEEN FOR C.C.C. I WOULD NOT HAVE BEEN EXPOSED TO ALL OF THESE EVENTS."

"I AM NOW OVER SIXTY-FIVE YEARS OF AGE, LIVED IN LOUISIANA ALL MY LIFE AND I AM JUST SEEING THE GOVENOR'S MANSION AND STATE CAPTOL FOR THE FTRST TIME."

"WORDS WILL NEVER BE ABLE TO EXPRESS THE IMPACT OF C.C.C. PROGRAMS ON OUR LIVES'

Time after time the itinerary included visits to cultural events scheduled at the two local universities: Grambling State University and Louisiana Tech. The participants also had an opportunity to visit the following:

Ballet- Swans on the Lake	Strand Theatre
Black History Parade	Shreveport, La.
Aquarium of the Americas	New Orleans, La.
Cruise-Mississippi River	New Orleans, La.
Old and New State Capitol	Baton Rouge. La.
Governor's Mansion	Baton Rouge, La.
Louisiana Arts and Science Center	Baton Rouge, La.

U.S.S. Kidd Museum	Baton Rouge, La.
Sci-Port Museum	Shreveport, La.
Louisiana State Fair Exhibits	Shreveport, La.
Louisiana State Museum	Shreveport, La.
IMAX Theatre	New Orleans, La.
Tuskegee University Tour	Tuskegee, Ala.
World of Coke	Atlanta, Ga.
A Ride on the Marta	Atlanta, Ga.
Jackson State University	Jackson, Ms.
Alabama State University	Montgomery, Ala.
Martin Luther King Center	Atlanta, Ga.
Underground Atlanta	Atlanta, Ga.
Tour of Colleges and Universities	Atlanta, Ga.
Birmingham Civil Rights Museum	Birmingham, Ala.
Six Flags Over Georgia	Atlanta, Ga.
Stone Mountain Riverboat Ride	Stone Mountain, Ga.
Car Museum	Shreveport, La.

The participants had numerous experiences during their travels and the amount of learning that took place can never be measured.

SPELLING BEE PROGRAM

The Spelling Bee Program is the "BRAINCHILD" of our state legislator, Pinkie Carolyn Wilkerson. We are now in our third year and the participation has increased each year. The purpose is to help students improve their spelling, increase their vocabularies, learn concepts, and develop correct English usage that will help them all their lives. High interest is created first on the local level, whereby students are invited to participate in the scheduled spelling bee for their town/city. The winner from each town/city advances to the area-wide spelling bee, which is rotated each year to one of the twelve towns involved. Because we are affiliated with the National Spelling Bee Program, the winner from the area-wide spelling bee advances to the Regional Spelling Bee in Shreveport, La. During the two years of our affiliation nationally, we have not had a winner to advance to the National Spelling Bee in Washington, D. C, which is the goal of the agency.

ACT PREPARATION WORKSHOP PROGRAM

The ACT Workshops are basically designed to help students to master the American College Test (ACT). As a result, the instructional component is designed to include a variety of diverse activities/strategies and resources /materials to enable the participants to increase their knowledge of the process of test-taking and the content covered on the different tests. The workshops are held in four of the centrally located towns- Arcadia, Bernice, Homer and Ruston, where participants are presented test-taking strategies and given an opportunity to apply the strategies to actual complete test items. The areas of concentration are Mathematics, Reading, English and Science. There are a variety of divers strategies used to meet the different learning styles and needs of the learner as related to the ACT competencies. Specifically, these strategies included on-going interactive sessions, teacher-directed development activities, and exercises involving the use of test-taking techniques.

ACADEMY PROGRAMS

The academy programs were held in each city/town nearby in order to eliminate the problem of travel for the participant& This program is designed (1) to provide intensive, interactive, educational and enriching experiences for youth ages 6-16; (2) to expose youth to innovative, creative activities that will make a difference in their lives and will enable them to know that they can make a significant contribution to society; (3) To empower youth to become self-sufficient and take their rightful places in society; and (4) to provide varied and meaningful experiences that will help to raise the level of self-esteem and encourage self-motivation.

The directors for each academy resided in the town/city, in which the academy was held, making it convenient to have numerous hands-on experiences for the familiar youth of the area. The academies placed emphasis on life skills, leadership, science, mathematics, entrepreneurship, medical technology, art and music. Community buildings/churches/schools are used for the sites. The academies have provided trips to the boyhood home of President Bill Clinton in Hope, Arkansas, Louisiana State University Medical Center in Shreveport, Sci-Port Museum in Shreveport, Monroe Civic Center for a religious drama, "Mahalia" and plans are now being made to carry academy participants to Baton Rouge, La., the site of the State Capitol.

MIMI-GRANT PROGRAMS

Three mini-grant programs have been awarded to three area church groups to provide tutorial programs, a quilting bee program, and a gardening program. Several of these programs are still in the initial stage of operation.

PROJECT GOLD PROGRAM

In an effort to expand its services and considering that the elderly population in Louisiana is presently that of about 500,000 people age 65 years and older and will double by the year 2025, the agency, along with impetus from Louisiana State Representative Pinkie Wilkerson (D-11), had the foresight and vision to implement a social cultural and recreational travel enrichment program for seniors. Project Gold (Giving Older Adults Longer Days) seeks to diversify and compliment the services being offered to the senior population in the parishes mentioned earlier. This program meets the social, cultural, and recreational travel enrichment needs of non-institutionalized senior population as well as improves their quality of life.

Activities and events involve short-day trips, the attendance to culturally entertaining and stimulating programs, and specifically planned "fun" days.

All in all, we feel that the programs herein describe support the literacy development efforts of the school and we firmly believe that the community must work hand in hand with the schools to help our youth and seniors achieve to their maximum. It is the desire of this agency to always collaborate with the home, church, school and any other agency to help promote literacy development.

CHAPTER 10

Tips and Techniques for Parents to
Enhance Literacy Learning

Sallie S. Evans
Lincoln Parish School Board
Ruston, LA

This chapter will discuss specific experiences and activities that parents can use at home to develop and reinforce literacy skins. The exercises are very practical and fun for parents to use with students.

The best way to ensure that your child will develop into a life-long reader is to instill in the child a love of words and a love for literature. Starting early when your child is an infant and continuing throughout the years that your child is under your supervision will enhance and enrich literacy efforts in the life of your child. This is the time to seize every oppom6ty to enrich your child's vocabulary with new words. Research has shown a strong connection between language development and learning to read. If your child is to understand what is said and can express thoughts effectively to others your child has a head start on reading. A child who has not been exposed to a wide variety of words will experience difficult understanding the words in print.

In order to develop and reinforce literacy skills, parents and family members must "Make Literacy A Family Affair". Families must make their home a literacy-rich environment filled with books, books and more books, great conversations, thought-provoking questions and tools for creative writing. The key is to start early. Don't wait on your child to start kindergarten, begin to "Read Right Now".

Parents and family members must demonstrate the importance placed on reading, by making reading a literacy thread that is a part of the family's daily activity.

STEPS TO LITERACY SUCCESS

Step I   *Fill your home with a variety of reading materials (books, magazines, newspapers, encyclopedias, etc). Let your child see you using these materials.*

Step 2   *Involve everyone in your household (toddler, young children, teens, and adults) in family reading time.*

Step 3   *Set aside a special time every day when everyone will stop, drop everything and read aloud to your child or let your child read to you.*

Step 4   *Be creative. Use different voices for each character. That makes it fun for everyone.*

Step 5   *Strengthen your child's communication skills through speaking in complete sentences and writing (ex.: Write thank you notes, letters to friends, grocery lists, addresses and telephone numbers, etc).*

Step 6   *Take the time to answer your child's questions, even if they interrupt the story. The idea is to make reading fun Reading to children ignites a love for words and for books.*

Step 7   *Take your child to the library regularly. Get them their own library card.*

Step 8   *Be a reading role model for your children. Have a TV-free night (no TV). Grab a book and read. "You must read to succeed!"*

PROVEN LITERACY EXPERIENCES AND ACTIVITIES

THAT WORK

Providing services to families and schools as Lincoln Parish School District's Parental Involvement and Preschool Coordinator and serving as President of the North LA Reading Council has afforded me the opportunity to be creative and innovative in designing, implementing and promoting literacy efforts in Lincoln Parish, surrounding parishes and throughout the state of Louisiana. Many positive experiences have been observed and documented as it relates to literacy program implementation.

In Lincoln Parish, thousands of families are exposed to free literacy services in the home through the monthly Parent and Child Activity Calendars. Developmentally appropriate literacy skills are made available to all families each month (September-August) that have children attending Title I Preschool programs. Families of children in grades K-6 receive monthly literacy activities, as well as, successful literacy strategies for families of children in grades 7-8. Preschool students additionally receive their own personalized books entitled *"What I Want To Be"* or *"All About Me"*. These books have a personalized picture enclosed of each child and will be a memoir for them, build their self-esteem and promote a love for books.

A literacy program that has reached into thousands of homes in the past four years is the Project F.R.E.D. (Families

Reading Every Day) Program. Included is a letter to parents and the monthly Project F.R.E.D. card.

TITLE I PARENTAL INVOLVEMENT HOME READING PROGRAM: PROJECT F.R.E.D. (FAMILIES READING EVERY DAY)

Dear Parents,

We invite you to join our Home Reading Program called "Project F.R.E.D." This program is sponsored through the Lincoln Parish Title I Parental Involvement Program. This special reading program provides an opportunity to develop a love for reading year round. This is a wonderful way to help your child to expand his/her reading skills, promote good reading habits and develop a stronger parent-child relationship.

It's easy to participate, plus, there's no cost to parents. All you have to do as a parent or family member is be willing to get involved for thirty (30) special minutes each day. We sincerely hope you will agree to read to your child, let your child read to you, or read along with your child every day. After "F.R.E.D. Time" each day make sure your child checks and dates the appropriate box on the color-coded reading card and you initial the box. A parent should initial each box, complete the address and telephone number. Parental signature is required.

When you and your child or children have read for a minimum of twenty-five (25) days each month, your child will receive a special certificate and a special award. The certificate and award may be picked up at the Title I Family Resource Center, 403 Kirkland Street, or at your child's school.

We are looking forward to starting our Home Reading Program with you and your family. For additional information about other programs families may get involved in, contact the Family Resource Center at (318) 255-7635.

Sincerely,

Sallie S. Evans,

Title I Parental Involvement/Pre-K Coordinator

The Title I Summer Enrichment Literacy Program has been outstanding. Students, teachers and their families have explored literacy and participated in journal writing through themes such as: *Summer Reading Safari, Star Search Read America, Go For the Gold Olympic Reading, Having a Whale of a Summer, Spouting Off About Extended Learning, Voyager Pre-Med, America Reads Challenge, and Read*Write*Now* activities for reading and writing Fun.

Through the North LA Reading Council, literacy efforts have been promoted through the Young Authors Contest, International

Literacy Day, Grandparents Day Activities, Newspaper In Education Week Activities, Children's Choice book selections, Read Across America (Dr. Seuss' Birthday), reading in the mall, Books for Tots distribution, mini workshops; and spring, summer and fall conferences promoting literacy.

As a presenter for the North LA Reading Council's Summer Conference in 1998, the theme "Early Literacy Connections: Ideas Teachers Can Share with Parents" was explored. To prepare for reading everyday try these 10 things to do with young children.

1.   *A little longer? When your child asks to stay up a little longer, say yes, and make it a 15 minute family reading opportunity.*

2.   *Reading pockets. Slip fun reading material into your pockets to bring home to your child-a story or comic strip, a greeting card, even a fortune cookie from lunch. Let your child know when there's something in your reading pocket.*

3.   *Phone home. Can't get away from the office? Keep a few children's books at work and instead of a coffee break, call home and use this opportunity to read to your child.*

4.   *Shop and read. Read aloud signs and labels in the supermarket. Putting away groceries is another great opportunity; even pre-readers can sort cans and boxes by colors and pictures.*

5. *Recipe for reading ingredients.* Jot down a favorite recipe on an index card, then read the ingredients together with your child as you both prepare a meal.

6. *Pack a snack, pack a book.* When you're going someplace with your child where there might be a long wait, bring along a bag of favorite books.

7. *Labels, labels, labels.* Label the objects in your children's room as they learn to name them. Add more labeled items from time to time.

8. *Look and listen.* Too tired to read aloud? By listening to a book on tape and turning the book pages with your children, you'll be reading with them.

9. *Better than TV.* Read a good action story or tale of adventure to replace an evening TV program.

10. *License to read.* On car trips, make it a game to point out and read vanity plates, license plates from different states, billboards, and interesting road signs.

TIPS TO ENCOURAGE CHILDREN TO READ AT HOME

At-Home Reading Tips

1. *In order to encourage success, set a good reading example for your children.* Be sure they have plenty of opportunities to see you enjoying reading.

2. *Make the public library a part of your children's lives.* *Check on special programs and activities that the library may offer to different age groups of children, including story hours, reading contests and discussions groups.*

3. *Use the library with your children.* *Help them to learn how to locate books with the help of librarians and catalog systems.* *Encourage enthusiasm by making your children feel proud of their selection of books.*

4. *Set aside a regular time for reading at home.* *It should be a time when the whole family can participate.*

5. *Read together.* *Select reading materials your children will enjoy.* *Try not to limit the types of materials.* *Use magazines, newspapers, comics, brochures and instructions as well as books.*

6. *Look over materials for words that may be unfamiliar to you or your children.* *When reading, pronounce the word and explain the meaning.* *Give your children a chance to read the word and explain it to you as well.*

7. *If time allows, have your children read the selection silently first, before reading it out loud.* *This will help them gain confidence and understand it better.*

8.   *Ask questions while reading.*   Start out with simple questions about the story. Later, ask questions that require an opinion or conclusion. Encourage your children to ask questions, also.

9.   *Share reading out loud with your children.* You can take turns reading paragraphs, sentences, or even whole books. If your child struggles with a word, tell him or her the word and continue. Be sure that this is a pleasant experience and not a difficult task for either you or your child.

10.   *Go over what you read with your children.* Let them tell you what they've read. Talk about what you each liked or disliked in what was read Try to remember and use any new words you read.

11.   *When you and your child finish reading together, encourage your children with praise.* Be enthusiastic about improvements as well as good work. A warm "thank you" with a smile and a hug can make a world of difference.

12.   *Be a positive Literacy Role Model for your children.* READ! READ! To Succeed, READ!

THINGS PARENTS CAN DO AT HOME TO HELP THEIR CHILD BECOME A BETTER LEARNER

* Read, Read, Read, to your children Have them read to your

* Accept your child as he is. Avoid comparing one child to

116

another.

* *Find out strengths and areas that need improvement.*
  BUILD ON STRENGTHS! WORK ON WEAKNESSES.
* *Reinforce what your child is working on in school*
* *Talk with your children.*
* *Listen to your children.*
* *Get and use a library card. It's free.*
* *Have newspapers and magazines handy and encourage children to look through them. Talk about the pictures.*
* *Discuss what your child learned each day (family round table, a la Evans).*
* *Praise children when they do a good job or try hard.*
* *Make sure your child gets sufficient rest/sleep so he/she is both mentally and physically ready to learn at school.*
* *Schedule a regular time for homework and/or reading. (Provide time, space, and help as required.)*
* *Stress the importance of getting a good education. (Make positive remarks in front of children.)*

CHAPTER 11

School Public Relations and Business Partnerships:
Key Components in the Development of Literacy Skills

Elaine Foster, Ph.D.
Tamara L. Roberts, Ph.D.
Grambling State University
Grambling, LA

School Public Relations: A Catalyst for Developing Business/Community Partnerships

School and business partnerships emerged over two decades ago as the result of sweeping educational reform. This collaboration began as a response to the public's outcry to improve our educational system. The landmark report, A Nation at Risk (1983), emphasized the decline of academic standards and student performance in America's schools and opened a floodgate of challenges for business leaders to take a more active role in revitalizing education. It is important for school business partnerships to continue to evolve and expand in order to facilitate the changes that significantly impact the overall education that all learners receive.

Partnership programs have traditionally focused mainly on short term, immediate goals that provide sorely needed human and material resources to schools (Whiteford, 1991). Today, these programs are considered to be vital components of the school's mission and curriculum. Breaking down the conventional walls of schools to include business resources have led to the development of creative educational programs that have increased student academic performance and improved the quality of instruction. This coalition has provided limitless opportunities to expand learning for students and to make learning relevant to student's lives. In areas where schools and businesses work together in educational partnerships, the students, schools and businesses are all beneficiaries of this joint effort.

One of the primary goals of school business partnerships is to integrate work-based learning experiences with classroom education in order to help prepare all students regardless of gender, race, or disability to enter the workforce or pursue secondary education (Holliday, 1990). The enactment of the School-to-Work Opportunities Act in 1994 prompted President Bill Clinton to urge the nation's schools and businesses to work together in a concerted effort to make workplace learning a key educational strategy. By working together, sharing in decision-making, and collaborating in the learning process, everyone wins.

120

It is more critical than ever that we market the importance of education to the business community (DeLapp & Schultz, 1996). Part of the trouble with the schools is that they do not have an effective and efficient means of communication with the public sector. To succeed in reforming schools, school administrators must first make an impression on that portion of the public that supports education. The business community needs to be aware of what is happening in the schools and how they can become effective agents of change in order to strengthen education. The school public relations plan is the best catalyst for informing the community about the positive educational gains that are being made in the nation's schools. Oftentimes, the attention is focused on media-inflated negative aspects of public education and the significant changes that make a difference in the quality of education for all students and educators become lost in the shuffle. To improve understanding and support from partners, schools must work diligently to shed the negative images that have overshadowed them for so long. It is essential for schools to showcase their best images before as many people as possible.

A well thought out public relations plan is the school's magnet for attracting business and community partners and for maintaining relationships of shared responsibility for education. The four basic public relation tenets, include 1) research, 2) action,

3) communication, and 4) evaluation must be clearly defined in order to ensure cooperation and collaboration from partners (Selvy, 1998). It is important for schools to be able to analyze where they stand in regards to partners they wants to reach, as well as develop goals, objectives, and strategies that go hand in hand with their mission. Additionally, it is important that schools carry out tactics necessary to meet the goals and objectives; and determine the effectiveness of the actions taken. By following these steps, schools can develop powerful vehicles for establishing effective business partnerships.

The school-based public relations program should be designed to strengthen business, community and education partnerships by making innovative school programs more visible to the community and more integrated with the community. This kind of collaboration can be accomplished through the incorporation of three public relations strategies, which include 1) publicity strategies that build and support promotion, 2) human relations strategies that focus on making contact with the "vital publics" or people important to the existence of the partnership program, and 3) community building strategies that emphasize the long range support of education in the community (Taunton & Carrington, 1991). The quality of education is enhanced when a close relationship exists between the school and the community.

The partnering of schools, businesses and communities represent a positive opportunity for progress. School public relations, is one of the most effective catalyst in educational reform.

The What and Why of Partnerships. School-business partnerships mushroomed in the 1980's as part of the Reagan administration's push for private sector initiatives. These partnerships functioned as a collaborative effort between schools, businesses and the community. They ranged from high level collaboration between major business leaders in a community and school executives to concentrated efforts by businesses to provide resources, school and work opportunities, and hands on experiences to students and teachers. The aim of partnering is to build public support for the improvement and restructuring of education.

Partnering is an important component of education. Throughout America, schools are making major attempts to increase the number of non-teacher adults who have some responsibility for promoting student learning and achievement. These alliances impact teaching and learning in various ways that empower all learners with academic and occupational skills needed for success in today's economy. School and business partners work together in many ways to advocate school reform changes and to initiate innovative programs that are essential to productive student outcomes. Partnerships enhance the relevance and quality of education for learners. By encouraging business and communities to take an active role in the learning process, a climate can be created in which everyone wins.

School-business partnerships are visible in many forms. They can be found in schools across the country but are more prevalent in schools with large student populations that are located in major cities (Clark, 1991). It is a common practice for some schools to have more than one business partner. In 1987-1988, 40% of the nation's public schools had a formal partnership with an external institution (Clark, 1991). Partnership programs focus on ways to improve certain school programs such as improving technology in the school or improving employability skills in students. These programs are of value to both schools and businesses. They are built on the premise that American business has much to lose if American schools fail (Clark, 1991).

There are many reasons for developing school business partnerships. They help to open the community as a classroom by bringing resources in and by helping teachers and students gain access to the larger community. The strength of the school is contingent upon the community. Community support is the driving force behind our nation's educational systems. Another reason to develop a partnership is that they have the potential to broaden opportunities for students. The human and material resources that businesses bring to students make classroom learning relevant and provide the support that makes it possible to focus on learning. To know that someone cares is important to teachers and students.

Business partners are the catalysts for educational reform. They have the potential to influence curriculum, instructional practices and methodology and the overall structure of the school. Business involvement can lead to changes that make schools efficient and effective. These partners serve as advocates within the community and with governing bodies that control what schools do.

The educational funding squeeze of the 1990's has brought the issue of education and business partnerships to the forefront. It is not the responsibility of partnerships to bear the financial burdens that bend and break the backs of public schools. However, the fiscal load is less difficult to carry when schools, businesses and communities band together in a concerted effort to improve education for all children. Many school programs would not be available to students without the financial contributions of partners.

Partnerships have made numerous valuable contributions to the education of students. Their interest in supporting students through various programs is one of the main reasons why businesses have become an important part of the partnering movement. Their support has led to significant changes and improvements throughout American schools. The way in which partners care about schools is reflected in the major impact they have made on public education. When teachers, students, and others view one another as partners in education, a caring community forms around students and begins it work (Epstein, 1992). Business partners are committed to educators to advocate change and to support new ideas. Educators who want better schools are actively seeking change and looking for partners who will remain committed to educating all children. Partnerships are beneficial to everyone.

The main reason to create partnerships is to help all students succeed in school and later on in life. Partnerships are valuable assets to the schools. They provide needed resources that enable teachers, administrators and school staff to improve the quality of learning for all students. They serve as change agents for restructuring school policies and programs. Businesses have a vested interest in education because schools supply the demand for competent workers who are the driving force of any kind of industry. Businesses are interested in improving the quality of education. It is important to know what a partnership is and to understand why there is a need for partnerships in order to develop a clear perception of the roles they play in public education.

The partnership movement has significantly increased over the past five years. It has been recognized as one of the most effective means of school support and reform. The status of the partnership concept soared to new heights with the signing of the School-to-Work Opportunities Act in 1994 by President Bill Clinton. This monumental legislative act was designed to support the development of work based learning programs by bringing schools and businesses together in partnerships. Schools were eager to implement these programs, however, the main difficulty was getting businesses involved. Businesses felt there was not enough self-interest to participate and the obstacles to participating were considerable (Bailey, 1995; Osterman, 1995; Stern, 1995). Companies believed that students could not contribute enough to justify the effort needed to supervise them (Bailey, 1995) and there were concerns about safety and liability.

To meet these challenges, schools must showcase their best images, using effective public relations strategies. One way to achieve public awareness and support is through a school based public relations campaign emphasizes bringing the public into the

127

schools, utilizing the local press, radio and television opportunities, and newsletters that focus on school and student success.

There are several types of public relations strategies which schools can use to generate public support and promotion. The aim of the promotion strategy is to gain attention and to make the community aware of what is going on in today's public schools. The most effective ways to get attention is through the use of exhibits, displays, posters, buttons and T-shirts. The building support strategy is based on the premise of delivered promises. The school provides evidence to verify that they are doing everything that has been agreed upon.

The human relations strategies focus on establishing a relationship with the "vital publics", or those partners who support education. These supporters are vital to the success of the partnership. The community-building strategy rests on the basic concept of long-range support from partners. The longevity of school business partnerships based on the outcomes of community involvement.

Public Relation Tips for Building School-Business Partnerships.

The key to successful school-business partnerships hinges on promoting educational programs to build community support. This can be accomplished by incorporating these simple strategies into the public relations program:

1) Join forces to discuss ways to improve the schools and the community they serve.

2) Define both the needs and the resources of all potential partners.

3) Secure commitments from all partners.

4) Develop a plan of action and set realistic priorities, goals and objectives.

5) Designate a primary contact person responsible for coordinating partnership activities in the school and the business.

6) Think big and long-term, but start small to ensure success.

7) Focus on acquiring human resources rather than on generating funds.

8) Evaluate the efforts of partners on a regular basis.

9) Recognize and appreciate the contributions of each partner.

10) Everyone involved should benefit from the partnership.

Conclusion. According to De Lapp and Schultz, it is more critical than ever that we market the importance of education to the community. If educators do not build support, involvement, and understanding, public confidence in education will continue to erode. It is up to school leaders, parents, elected officials, the business community and the general public to realize that schools are an excellent investment in the future with a high rate of return.

Promoting schools to businesses and the community, conveying accurate information to them and soliciting information from the community are attributes of an excellent public relations program. Drawing upon human resources in the community can tap an unlimited source of supplementary educational experiences for students. School public relations are the foundation for effective school business/community relationships. The strength of the partnership is contingent upon the effectiveness of the Public Relation Program.

References

Bailey, T. R. (1995). Incentives for Employer Participation in School-to-Work Programs. In learning to work: Employer involvement in school-to-work transition programs. Washington, DC: Brookings Institution.

Clark, T. (1991). Collaboration to build competence: The Urban. Washington, DC: U.S. Government Printing Office.

Epstein, J. (1992). School and family partnerships: Career-long growth, development and reform. University Park, PA: University Council for Educational Administration.

Goble, N. (1993, December). School-community relations: New for the '90s. Education Digest, 59(4), 45.

Holliday, A.E., (1990). Revise the scope of your public relations program to enhance student achievement. Journal of Educational Public Relations, 12(4), 4-5.

A Nation at Risk: The Imperative for Educational Reform. Washington, DC: National Commission on Excellence in Education, U.S. Department of Education, 1983.

Osterman, P. (1995). Involving employers in school-to-work programs. In T. Bailey's (Ed.), Learning to work: Employer involvement in school-to-work transition programs. Washington, DC: Brookings Institution.

Schultz, B., DeLapp, T. (1996, November/December) School Publicity. Thrust for Educational Leadership, 26 (3), 10.

Selvy, G. (1996). Seven tips for building better school business-partnerships. Techniques: Making Education & Career Connections, 73, 41-42.

Stem, D. (1995). Employer options for participation in school-to-work programs. In T. Bailey's (Ed.), Learning to work: Employer involvement in school-to-work transition programs. Washington, DC: Brookings Institution.

Taunton, M. and Carrington, D.M. (1991). PR Strategies for a school arts support campaign in the community. Journal of Educational Public Relations, 7, 5-9,

Whiteford, L. (1991). School Business Partnerships. Journal of Educational Public Relations, 15, 4-9.

CHAPTER 12

Making Connections: A Field-Based Model for Preparing Pre-Service Teachers to Promote Literacy Learning

Loretta Walton Jaggers, Ed. D.
Andolyn Brown Harrison, Ph.D.
Vicki Renee Brown, Ph. D.
Grambling State University
Grambling, LA

Jean G. Brown, M.Ed.
Louisiana Reading Association

INTRODUCTION

A review of the literature indicates that teacher preparation programs should include diverse and consistent opportunities for students to make connections between theory and practice. As a result, the Teacher Education Department at Grambling State University provides numerous field-based experiences for students to make connections between course content and actual classroom instruction. These experiences allow students to use reflective thinking as they discuss realistic situations in the classroom with basic theory.

More specifically, Grambling State University's Teacher Education Department was involved in a K-3 collaborative project, which involved observation-participation activities for pre-service students at an elementary school near the Grambling campus. The Teacher Education majors were enrolled in a Reading Methodology course (ED 431: Diagnosis and Correction of Reading Difficulties), for the Spring Semester 1999. The course met on Tuesday and Thursday from 9:30 AM to 10:45 AM. One day was designed for the discussion of basic concepts and theory and the other day was designed for direct involvement in the classroom with students and a supervising teacher. Prior to starting at the on-site school, the course instructor arranged several meetings with the building principal, other school administrators, and supervising teachers. The students were placed in K-3 classrooms at the elementary school. They initially observed and conferred with the supervising teachers to help identify the needs of the students that they would be working with. The university students used both formal and informal means of diagnosis to aid in the development of the remediation strategies and resources. Afterwards, they designed and presented creative strategies and materials to remediate the learner needs. The process served to help students make connections between the theory presented and discussed in the university class with the practical application at the on-site school.

Course Design

The course was composed of two basic components. Component I involved the introduction and discussion of diverse formal and informal procedures for diagnosing reading difficulties. After the background information or course foundation was discussed, then the different types of formal procedures (standardized tests, Informal Reading Inventories), and informal procedures (writing sample, attitude inventory, interest inventory, classroom observation, teacher interview, daily work) were presented and examined. Component II involved the development of creative lessons and materials for remediating the reading difficulties that were identified from the battery of diagnostic procedures. As a result of the basic course goals, the students were involved in three basic experiences. First, the college students were asked to observe the basic management and operation of the Reading/Literacy program in their assigned classroom. Second, they were asked to administer some informal and formal diagnostic procedures that were discussed in the university class. Third, they had to review all of the results of the diagnostic procedures that were used to determine the Literacy/Reading needs of the student that they had been assigned. As a result, each university student was asked to design a specific *Remediation Packet* for their assigned student. The *Remediation Packet* included creative materials and activities for remediating the specific skill(s) of their assigned student. The university students had an opportunity to share their classroom experiences during their university class period on Thursday. The course instructor monitored each university student very carefully while they were working in the classrooms at the on-site school.

Course Format

Behavioral Objectives

After completion of this course, the student will:

- Review and explain the "process" of reading skill development.
- Define and identify the sequence of each category of reading skill development
- Define specific terminology related to diagnosis and remediation of reading difficulties.
- Identify and use formal and informal procedures for diagnosis.
- Design, identify, and use varied activities, strategies, and resources for the correction and remediation of reading difficulties.
- Discuss diagnostic and remediation procedures for the special

needs learner.

- Identify the role of the parents in the diagnostic and remediation process.

- Explain the role of the classroom teacher/school personnel, reading specialist, the administration, and the parent/community in the diagnostic and remediation process.

- Demonstrate the use of materials, activities, and remediation. strategies which may be used for promoting *education that is multicultural.*

- Design a Diagnostic-Remediation Packet, which will be used with a student in the on- site school.

- Design and participate in a Reading Seminar, which demonstrates the role of the home, school and community in supporting literacy learning.

- Participate in diverse field-based experiences which relate to the improvement of literacy learning.

- Identify the role of technology in the diagnosis and remediation process.

- List and explain the types of reading difficulties.

- Explain characteristics of "classroom diagnosis and clinical diagnosis".

- Identify reading difficulties and strategies for remediation in the content areas.

Course Content Outline

- Introduction
  - Student expectations
  - Teacher expectations
  - Course expectations
- Background Information
  - Reading defined
  - The sequence of reading/literacy skills
  - Types of reading difficulties
- The Nature of Diagnosis and Evaluation
  - Diagnosis defined
  - Guidelines for diagnosis
  - Formal procedures
  - Informal procedures
  - Assessment and evaluation
  - The relation between diagnosis and remediation
- Remediation and correcting reading difficulties
  - Strategies and activities
  - Materials and resources
  - The role of technology

- Diagnosis and Remediation

  -The Special Needs Learner

  -Instruments and procedures

  - Strategies for remediation
- Parental/Community Involvement in the Diagnosis and Remediation Program

  -Parent interviews

  -Community resources

  -Promoting involvement
- The Role of the Classroom Teacher/School Personnel, Administrator, Parent/Community in the Diagnostic Remediation Process

  -Team Approach

  -Relating Diagnosis to Corrective Procedures
- The Role of Multicultural Education in the Diagnostic Remediation Process

  -Materials for diagnosis, assessment, and evaluation

  -Learning style/reading style - teaching style

  -Strategies and activities for remediation
- Addressing Reading Difficulties in the Content Areas

  -Materials for diagnosis

  -Strategies of remediation
- Summary

139

Major text:

Wilson, R. (1996). Diagnostic and remedial reading for classroom and clinic. Columbus, OH: Merrill Publishing.

Implementation/ Application

The field-based experiences that the Teacher Education majors were involved in provided numerous opportunities for them to make a connection between theory and practice. First, they had an opportunity to research and discuss varies procedures for diagnosing and assessing reading difficulties, then they had an opportunity to use the techniques in an actual classroom setting with students. Since this course also deals with remediating reading difficulties, the field-based experiences gave the university students an opportunity to first administer diagnostic procedures. Then, based on the results of their student, they designed and presented remediation strategies in the classroom with their assigned elementary student. Since the course requirements include the development and implementation of a *Diagnostic-Remediation Packet*, the university students had an opportunity to use diverse resources/materials to *tailor* the corrective strategies and materials to the specific needs of the student. Some of these included commercial and teacher-made materials. The university students also completed article critiques, which they discussed during the university class periods. These article critiques also related to specific topics on the course content outline, which enhanced the understanding of the diagnosis remediation process. This activity provided an opportunity for the university students to relate textbook information to current trends and actual classroom application at the on-site school. In effort to reinforce basic concepts and clarify ideas, the university students maintained *Inquiry Journals.* They had an opportunity to share notes regarding their actual classroom experiences with the children as related to principles and practices of diagnosis and remediation.

The *Inquiry Journals* were submitted to the course instructor at specific periods during the semester. The university students also had an opportunity to share specific observation/participation experiences that related to information presented during the class discussions. The *Inquiry Journals* focused on the following:

- Procedures used to organize activities for Reading instruction
- Motivational techniques for presenting the lesson and involving the students in the instructional process
- Use of instructional materials/ resources which focus on the diverse needs of learners

- The physical setting and classroom environment
- Techniques used to diagnose, assess, and/or evaluate Reading performance
- Techniques used to enhance positive self-concept development
- Strategies used to promote literacy skills (writing, listening, speaking, thinking, reading) and enhance test-taking skills
- The administration of a Diagnostic Packet to help determine the strengths and needs of the assigned student in the classroom (ED 431 student)
- The summary of one interview with the cooperating teacher to help determine the needs of the assigned students (ED 431 student)
- Tutoring experiences for the assigned student (ED 431 student)

Model Feedback

ED 431 Instructor Testimonial

I was extremely pleased to have an opportunity to teach this field-based class at the on-site school. There was a great deal of cooperation from the administration and teachers. Although the Teacher Education Department at Grambling provides numerous opportunities for diverse field-based experiences, this class was held at the school where the students observed and participated. They had an opportunity to see the operation of the entire school setting in relationship to the course objectives and previous courses. Specifically, they had an opportunity to see how the "Big 3" (the principal, the teachers, and the community/parents) can work together to promote the success of the students. They had an opportunity to observe strategies that teachers used to promote self-esteem and literacy across the curriculum as they taught the content concepts. They also had an opportunity to observe specific techniques that the teachers used to organize, manage, and control their individual classrooms. More importantly, the students who were exposed to this model expressed that this experience provided direct hands-on involvement and gave them an opportunity to interact with the students, supervising teachers, and principal. Last and certainly not least, these experiences give the students an opportunity to administer individual tests to students and observe some of the supervising teachers administer the DRA (Direct Reading Assessment). Finally, the university students had an opportunity to truly make the connection as they observed the school setting, interacted with the principal and teachers, and planned and presented instructional strategies based on careful assessment.

Loretta Walton Jaggers,
Teacher Education Department (GSU)

Testimonials of Students Enrolled in ED 431

As a pre-service teacher, I feel that this field -based experience has had a positive impact on me. I was assigned to a kindergarten class at the on-site school. This opportunity gave me hands-on experiences that I need to become a more successful and enthusiastic teacher. I have observed several classrooms and I have recognized that it is truly one thing to know the skills and another to be able to successfully implement them in the classroom.

All of the information that I have learned has shown me some of the things to expect when I start teaching. I also observed the different strategies that that teachers use to promote a "print-rich" environment in the classroom. This experience also helped me to feel more secure about teaching as I prepare to go into the *world of work.* I was also very proud to see the *team approach* that was practiced at the school. I think that this was a wonderful experience that every pre-service teacher should be exposed to.

Rakia Veal

I am extremely pleased to have had the opportunity to participate in this field-based program. By participating in this experience, I am able to interact one-on-one with the principal, the

144

teacher, and the students. I now have the ability to practice the skills learned in my Diagnosis and Correction class. The program enabled me to *get the feel* of an actual classroom, teach lessons, and specifically assess the needs of the students. This is a very worthwhile program because it gave me the opportunity to interact with other students outside of the immediate area. This means that I am also able to see the similarities and differences between school districts. From this class, I know that I will have learned a vast array of knowledge.

Nyva Hammonds

I feel that this field-based involvement is a positive experience for me as a pre-service teacher. I was assigned to a first grade class. This experience gave me the opportunity to be exposed to additional hands-on experiences that I need to become a successful teacher. Learning the different techniques and procedures in a university course is one thing, but actually getting the opportunity to apply the skills in a "real" classroom is another valuable learning experience.

This field-based program also provides an opportunity for direct interaction with the students, classroom teacher, and building principal. Additionally, I had an opportunity to observe different learning styles and reading styles, as related to the use of diverse instructional strategies. The techniques that were applied in the classroom gave me many creative ideas that I can implement in my own classroom.

As a result of my involvement in this experience, I am now sure that this is the profession that I'm destined to be in.

Crystal Cooley

ED 431 serves as a "real life experience". The university class interacts with our assigned on-site classes. We participated in numerous activities, which helped to strengthen my understanding of some of the current trends and practices in the area of literacy/reading. I especially enjoyed designing the creative literature-based activity, which my class enjoyed.

The previous reading course, (ED 303), served as an excellent foundation for understanding and relating to the experiences that were involved in this course. Knowledge of the reading process and related literacy skills made it easier for me to understand all of the factors that impact the diagnosis and correction process. Now I am able to better understand the importance of using proper assessment, planning carefully, and teaching to the needs of our students.

Veneta Carter

The program at the on-site school was quite a rewarding experience. I worked with Mrs. Williams and Mrs. Bradley. Both are excellent teachers with excellent classrooms. The administration interacts in a positive and supportive manner with the students as well as the teachers. I was so impressed with the overall organization of the program.

Being a student at Grambling State University is a reward within itself. I particularly enjoyed having the opportunity to go into the community for hands-on training. Over the past week I have had the opportunity to work with two students in Mrs. Bradley's classroom. The two students have difficulty reading material at their level. My goal is to greatly enhance the reading performance of these students by the end of the school term.

This program re-emphasized the importance of setting goals and high expectations for the students. I hope that other students will be able to benefit from this program as much as I did in the future.

Melony Harris

Field-based experiences should be designed to enhance the teaching/learning process for teacher educators. I can truly say that this experience has truly done that for me. I am now able to make connections between the reading skills and actual classroom application.

This course, *Diagnosis and Correction*, has established a purpose of its own. It is our role as effective teachers to diagnose and remediate to the best of our ability. This course has provided a wealth of information and experiences for us to do just that. In addition to the specific course objectives, I have gained other information. Some of which include, classroom management strategies, strategies for promoting positive principal-teacher-student relationships. Moreover, this training has given me the opportunity to interact easier with my students. I especially enjoyed the Diagnostic-Assessment Packet, which provided more insight on the assessment-instruction connection.

Reyna Teamer-Robertson

The field-based experience provided an opportunity for me to be involved with the principal, teacher and the students on an on-going basis. This program provides an excellent opportunity to enhance the teaching/learning process. It helps to get pre-service teachers ready for students and the whole school environment. Finally, this program also stresses the importance of time management skills that are needed to help one to become an effective teacher.

Ernest Sterling

I believe that the program will be very helpful to me. It has provided some additional hands-on experiences for me with elementary students. This experience allowed me to see the class from a teacher's perspective. This program will also allow me to incorporate what I learn in ED 431 in my classroom on a regular basis. I am grateful that the on-site school allowed us to gain the experience that we all need as pre-service teachers.

Ronald Coleman

Going to the on-site school, teaching lessons, and assisting with the education process of students was an extremely rewarding experience for me. The involvement with the class helped me to see what type of methods and materials that I might use in my own classroom. Also, I was very proud to be a positive role model for the children. I enjoyed seeing the children's faces as I taught them and interacted with them.

Craig Jones

As a pre-service teacher, I feel it is necessary that I am provided hands-on training in actual classroom settings. This experience allows me the chance to work with the teacher and students. During the field-based experience, I had the opportunity to apply the knowledge I have learned. I am very thankful for this experience and believe that I will greatly benefit from this experience.

Keyshera Kirk

Summary

As a result of the feedback from the program participants, this model provided invaluable experiences and opportunities for all persons involved. The university students also had an opportunity to draw from the experiences from other university classes as they expanded their knowledge about diagnosis and remediation. Through their classroom involvement at the on-site school, the university students had an opportunity to strengthen their own self-confidence as they worked with students, teachers, administrators, and community representatives.

CHAPTER 13

Strengthening Literacy Skills Across the Core Curricula by Addressing Individual Differences

Glenda S. Starr, Ph.D.,
Grambling State University
Grambling, LA

Donald W. Smith, Ed.D.
Monroe City Schools
Monroe, LA

Throughout the past twenty years the author repeatedly observed numerous in service teachers who did not sufficiently accommodate individual differences. Far too many students are unintentionally left out of activities because the teacher fails to vary methods of delivery and materials to accommodate learning styles. Lessons would have been more accommodating if teachers had combined the application of oral, visual and kinesthetic activities and materials to teach concepts. Teachers should obtain a class profile prior to meeting the class in order to learn about the demographical background of prospective students. This information will provide the most pronounced differences, which exist among students.

When planning instruction for a class, a teacher must identify the differences among the students in the group. Those differences are: Differences in Mental Ability, Differences in Achievement, Differences in Sociability, Differences in Maturation, Differences in Experience, Differences in Interests, Differences in Motivation and Differences in Learning Styles. According to Barth (1990) teaching exists as an exciting and energizing profession with many rewards. In particular, teachers derive significant rewards from meeting the needs of diverse learners. Since students from our nation's more than one hundred racial and ethnic groups with special needs are increasing in number, effective teachers recognize that their classrooms are enriched by these varied backgrounds. To experience the satisfaction of helping all students learn, consideration must be given to student variability (differences among students in regard to their developmental needs, interests, abilities, and disabilities) and student diversity (differences among students in regard to gender, race ethnicity, culture, and socioeconomic status). An appreciation for such diversity will help teachers to experience the rewards that come from enabling each student to make his or her unique contribution to classroom life (p. 39).

152

The Carnegie Forum on Education and the Economy (1986) provides an inclusive description of how teachers should prepare for the profession. Teachers should have a good grasp of the ways in which all kinds of physical and social systems work; a feeling for what data are and the uses to which they can be put; and ability to help students see patterns of meaning where others see only confusion; an ability to foster genuine creativity in students; and the ability to work with other people in work groups that decide for themselves how to get the job done. They must be able to learn all the time, as the knowledge required to do their work twists and turns with new challenges and the progress of science and technology. Teachers must think for themselves if they are to help others, render critical judgment. They must be people whose knowledge is wide ranging and whose understanding runs deep (p. 25).

Arthur Wise (1995), President of the National Council for the Accreditation of Teacher Education states that as teachers address the individual differences of their students, they should be cautious about their own reactions to their students. When teachers communicate their expectations and observe students' reactions and performances, they tend to behave differently toward those students for whom they hold high and low expectations

(p. 6). Table One reflects teacher differential treatment of high and low achievers. No matter what the individual differences may be, the goal of the teacher should be to educate all students to the best of the students' capabilities. Different students need different things. Some may need individual personal attention from instructors. Grant and Secada (1990) write that for some students personalized education may involve opportunities for independent study, for work in student-led groups or for other types of learning involving less rather than more individual contact with others. Even though students have well-practiced ways of learning and coping with different kinds of instruction, they still learn materials differently (p. 31).

Table 1

<u>Teacher Differential Treatment of High and Low Students</u>

<u>Categories of Behavior</u>

<u>Categories of Behavior</u>	Teacher Behaviors
Praise and feedback	Rewarding inappropriate behaviors by lows. Criticizing lows more often than highs for failure. Praising lows less frequently than highs for success. Briefer and less informative feedback to questions of lows.
Verbal interactions	Waiting less time for lows to answer. Giving lows answers or calling on someone else. Calling on lows less often to respond to questions.
Interpersonal interactions	Generally paying less attention to lows. Interacting with lows less frequently. Demanding less from lows. Interacting with lows more privately than publicly. Seating lows farther away from the teacher.
Instructional strategies	Less use of effective but time consuming methods with lows. More seatwork and low-level academic tasks for lows. Leaving lows out of some instructional activities.

155

Note: A reflection of differential categories of behavior between
          students and teachers. From Looking in classrooms by T. L.
          Good & J. E. Brophy. (1987). 128-129.

In order to effectively address individual differences, teachers should integrate traditional and nontraditional resources. One of the proven education tools is Bloom's Taxonomy. According to Rosenshine (1992), the major purpose in constructing a taxonomy of educational objectives is to facilitate communication. Another important purpose is to plan lessons, which will accommodate the individual difference of students. Bloom's taxonomy was constructed to move students through different levels of learning. Those six well-known levels are: 1.00 Knowledge; 2.00 Comprehension; 3.00 Application; 4.00 Analysis; 5.00 Synthesis; 6.00 Evaluation. Some students move upward through to level 5.00 Synthesis and 6.00 Evaluation with some ease. However, other students may never get past levels 2.00 Comprehension or 3.00 Application (p. 33). Teachers may use Bloom's taxonomy as a focal point for planning individualized instruction (p. 41). Table 2 shows the format of Bloom's Taxonomy.

Educators have used Bloom's Taxonomy as a resource for years. In fact, Bloom's Taxonomy was a major source in most teacher preparation training. Presently, it provides a resourceful tool in the training of pre-service teachers. Bloom's Taxonomy serves as an excellent example of a traditional resource, which lends itself for application in planning nontraditional lessons. Skillfully used, Bloom's Taxonomy stimulates higher order thinking creativity and provocation toward inquiry learning.

Table 2

Six Major Levels of Bloom's Taxonomy

Level	Characteristic Student Behaviors
Knowledge	Remembering; memorizing; recognizing; recalling
Comprehension	Interpreting; translating from one medium to another; describing in one's own words
Application	Problem-solving; applying information to produce some result
Analysis	Subdividing something to show how it is put together; finding the underlying structure of communication; identifying motives
Synthesis	Creating a unique, original product that may be in verbal form or may be a physical object
Evaluation	Making a value decision about issues; resolving controversies or differences of opinion

Note: *Cognitive Behaviors from simple to complex behaviors. From Taxonomy of Educational Objectives: The Classification of Educational Goals. Handbook 1: The Cognitive Domain, edited by Benjamin S. Bloom, et al. (p.110, 1986).*

158

Teachers should maintain a current library of proven strategies for addressing individual differences. However, the following student characteristics should always be considered.

Student Characteristics

- Intelligence. Siegel and Siegel (1984) write that intelligent students do better than less intelligent students in most educational situations. It does make a difference how students of differing intelligence are taught. Bright students will generally be able to handle a greater information-processing load than less able student; that is, the able students can figure out things better for themselves and provide their own organization. The less able students are more likely to benefit from attempts to simplify and organize the material for the students, organization that may be detrimental for the better student (p. 118).

- Cognitive style. Some students are predisposed to learn facts; others are disposed to apply and synthesize facts. According to Siegel and Siegel (1984), in an experiment at Miami University, the former type of student was particularly helped by personal contact with the instructor. In addition, students with little prior knowledge in a subject matter area also benefited particularly from personal contact with the teachers (p. 121). In a later publication,

159

however, Siegel and Siegel (1986), point out that the effect of personal contact with instructors depends upon what the instructor does (p. 12).

- Authoritarianism. Watson (1986) studies the effect of permissive and restrictive teaching and testing methods upon students differing in authoritarianism and permeability (extroversion). The methods were not differently effective as measured by achievement tests, but student satisfaction was affected by testing methods. Highest satisfaction resulted when students were tested in an atmosphere appropriate for their needs; that is, permissive for permeable, restrictive for impermeable. This finding is in line with the finding of Hountras (1990) that authoritarian students prefer a high degree of departmental control of instruction (p. 83).

- Motivation. Students display specific motives for learning. Students who accept responsibility for their own learning tend to be high in the achievement motive. Koenig (1990) similarly finds that women high in need for affiliation do better work in classes where the teacher takes a personal interest in students; conversely, men who are low in need for affiliation tend to relatively poorly in these classes (p.31). Beach (1990) studies the personality variable of

160

sociability as a predictor of achievement in lecture and small-group teaching methods. In the lecture session the non-sociable students (as measured by the Guilford Inventory of Factors STDCR) achieve significantly more than the sociable students; in the small-group sections the results were reversed. Personal contact with the instructor is valuable for some students, but not for all. Those likely to be favorably affected are those with low motivation and those high in sociability or need for affiliation. There are many students who fall in these groups, but also many who are not positively affected and may even achieve less when personal contact with the instructor is increased (p. 101).

- Anxiety. What is the effect of anxiety upon learning? How can you best teach anxious students? The answers to these questions turn out to be less obvious than one would expect. Generally, psychologists assume that anxiety is detrimental to learning. The research evidence suggests that the relationship is more complex, depending equally on the level of anxiety, the difficulty of the material, and the ability of the student. Since anxiety is generally believed to be increased by uncertainty, the anxious person should work most effectively in a highly structured situation. This hypothesis is partially supported by Smith (1991), who finds that anxious students who are permeable (sensitive to stimuli, impulsive, socially oriented, and low in ego strength) make optimal progress in remedial reading course when taught by directive methods. Impermeable anxious students, however, are unaffected by differences in teaching methods (p. 51).

- Introversion-extroversion. Leith (1984) carries out experiments and reviews a number of students on differential effects of various educational situations on introverts and extroverts. In his discussion of the "learning cell", 46 extroverts learn better when studying with another extrovert than when working alone, Leith also finds that extroverts learn better by a discovery method, while introverts learn better by reception. Similarly, extroverts learn better with less feedback, while introverts learn better with more feedback (p. 17).

- Sex. The coeducational institutions may have a vested interest in the assumption that the best education for men is also best for women. In any case, until recently very little research has dealt with the differences in learning styles of men and women. Carrier (1987) investigates the manner in which individual differences in four personality variables

162

affected performance in more and less stressful testing situations. He finds that one of the most important variables determining reaction in his experiment was sex. Women were much more detrimentally affected than men by stress situations (p. 9).

In later experiment McKeachie (1988), reveals that half of the students in a large class received a tranquilizing drug, meprobamate, while the other half received a placebo just before an examination. If students tend to be too anxious, such a drug should improve test scores. The results did not confirm this hypothesis. Students who had the drug reported experiencing less anxiety during the examination than did the placebo group, but they did not make better scores The really interesting result of the experiment resulted in the sex-drug interaction Women benefited from the drug more than men. Sex once again turned out to be an important variable. The results make sense if a curvilinear relationship between anxiety and performance is assumed, with women too anxious and men less than optimally anxious. Reduced anxiety should result in improved performance for women, but poorer performance for men. Once again, teaching techniques have shown different effects on different types of students (p. 17)

• Student-discipline interactions. McKeachie (1988) adds the characteristic learning problems differ somewhat from discipline to discipline, and the general student characteristics may be far less important in individualizing instruction than student characteristics related to hang-up in particular disciplines. For example, in mathematics a relevant characteristic may be the student's attitude toward mathematics, their previous success in it. For women, performance may reflect the degree to which mathematics is seen as a masculine activity (pp. 17-18).

In essence, literacy skills may be strengthened across the core curricula by addressing individual differences. Even though students may learn in varying ways; they do learn. The awareness of variations in learning enables the teacher to prepare productive lessons, which will stimulate and enhance the entire learning environment. Whether the differences in students are obvious in mental ability, achievement, sociability, maturation, experiences, interests or maturation, the main purpose is the accomplishment of the end product - *Learning Productivity.*

References

Barth, R. (1990). Improving Schools from within. San Francisco: Jossey-Bass

Beach, L. R. (1990). Sociability and academic achievement in various types of learning situations. Journal of Educational Psychology, 21, (3), 91-93.

Carnegie Forum on Education and Economy (1986). A nation prepared: Teachers for the twenty-first century. New York: Author Press.

Grant, C.A., & Secada, W.G. (1990). Preparing teachers for diversity, Handbook of Research on Teacher Education. New York: Macmillan.

Koenig, P. (1990). Personality, academic profile and independent study. Journal of Education Psychology, 50, (2), 132-134.

Leith, G. (1984). Conflict and interference: studies of the facilitating effects of reviews in learning sequences. Programmed Learning and Educational Technology, 8, 41-442.

McKeachie, H. J. (1988). Teaching tips: A Guidebook for the beginning college teacher. Lexington, Massachusetts: D.C. Heath and Company.

Rosenshine, B. (1992). The use of scaffolds for teaching higher-level cognitive strategies. Educational Leadership, 27(3), 26-29.

Siegel, L., & Siegel, L. C. (1984). Retention of subject matter as a function of large-group instructional procedures. Journal of Educational Psychology, 51(2), 69-71.

Smith, H. (1991). Eco-system project. Educational Connections, 11(1), 7-8.

Watson, J. B. (1986). Behaviorism. New York: People's Institute.

Wise, A. E. (I 995). Legislated learning revisited. Phi Delta Kappan, 69(5), 61-63.

CHAPTER 14

Preparing Teachers To Work With Diverse
Student Populations

Marilyn M. Irving
Howard University
Washington, DC

This chapter focuses on some of the responsibilities schools, colleges, and departments of education must assume to prepare all teachers to teach and work with diverse student populations. Given changes in the demographic composition of the teaching force in the next decade, this chapter addresses some fundamental recommendations for revising the curriculum and structure of pre-service teacher education programs so that all teachers will be able to teach every child in any situation.

The student population of today's schools reflects widely diverse socioeconomic, linguistic, and ethnic backgrounds, yet few teacher training programs are currently addressing the need to recruit and train teachers reflecting this diversity. Academic preparation at the undergraduate and graduate level is critical that teachers be exposed to a wide variety of liberal arts and education courses during heir undergraduate and graduate training. It is important that teachers are trained well because after all they must impart substantive knowledge to elementary and secondary students. Such knowledge has been mastered by prospective teachers; they are then ready to link theory to practice when they begin to teach.

When becoming familiar with specific foundations and behavioral aspects of teaching, they also become familiar with a variety of methodological techniques. They must also be award that teaching is also influenced be factors such as racial and cultural backgrounds, the ability and motivational levels of the students, the setting of the school (for example, rural, urban, or suburban), adequacy of instructional resources (for example, textbooks, equipment, laboratories, and so on), class size, and so on. For those reasons, the professional preparation of pre-service teachers must include additional academic knowledge related to diversity and diverse contexts that can be incorporated into their professional education curricula and clinical experiences. Being aware of that knowledge, novice teachers will be better equipped to successfully teach children who come from culturally, racially, and socio-economically diverse backgrounds.

Because of the challenges created by adverse social and economic conditions in the world today, tomorrows cohort of teachers will need to be more proficient in many more skills than

168

are teachers who were trained over the last two decades. More children--particularly in public schools--come from poorer backgrounds. Because of smaller budgets in most school districts, class size is larger today, which places greater responsibilities on teachers who must work with limited resources. Teachers of the future will have to be creative and resourceful educational leaders who are independent thinkers, who can successfully implement instructional practices.

Besides being knowledgeable in many content areas, future teachers must also become more competent in a variety of methodological techniques so that they can adapt and modify those skills to meet the individual needs of their students. These teachers must also be flexible and knowledgeable enough to use alternative instructional practices when their students are not achieving successfully. Teachers of today's culturally diverse classrooms must know how to plan and organize effective instructional situations, how to motivate students and manage their classrooms, and how to motivate students, in addition to being competent in the assessment of the academic strengths and weaknesses of all children; and learn how to encourage the cooperation of their students' families and communities in the conduct of their daily responsibilities (Garibaldi, 1991).

One of the areas to which pre-service teaches need more exposure to is the cultural differences that exist between and among students. This is an important dimension since a great deal of research over the last decade has shown that children from culturally diverse backgrounds do indeed exhibit learning differences and that other factors such as parental support, encouragement, and feedback positively affect their motivation, aspirations, and achievement (Boykin, 1979; Hale-Benson, 1986- Clark, 1983- Oakes, 1985; Willis 1999).

Teachers of culturally different children, therefore, must recognize that learning distinctions are prevalent and that environmental influences can mediate academic success. A variety of techniques have been used in schools, college and departments of education to increase education majors' awareness of and sensitivity toward students of different racial, cultural and ethnic backgrounds.

To be effective educators, teachers must be highly competent in planning and organizing instruction as well as in managing the classroom environment if their students are to be academically successful. Some of these management skills are learned in methods courses, others are developed in educational psychology and social foundations of education courses, and still other expertise is derived from exposure to classroom situations in schools through clinical and practical experiences.

Recognition and understanding of contextual factors are extremely important in successful teaching practices, and those factors influence the planning and organization of instruction. An inter-organizational report of the American Association of Colleges for Teacher Education, the American Federation of Teachers, the National Council on Measurement in Education, and the National Education Association identifies four key skills that teachers must possess prior to engaging in instruction: "understanding students' cultural backgrounds, interests, skills, and abilities as they apply across a range of learning domains and/or subject areas; understanding students' motivations and their interests in specific class content; clarifying and articulating the performance outcomes expected of pupils; and planning instruction for individuals or groups of students" *(Standards for Teacher Competence in the Educational Assessment of students, 1989, p. 2)*.

Pre-service teachers must, therefore, be trained to employ approaches and modalities that accommodate the distinctive learning styles of students from different racial and cultural groups. While traditional approaches may be useful in some settings, teachers must be able to adapt or select the pedagogy that is most

171

appropriate. Research on cooperative learning practices indicates that students achieve more when working in groups rather than working individually or in competitive situations (Johnson and Johnson 1989).

The teacher who bases lesson planning on his or her desired educational goals and objectives, who is highly organized, and who varies learning strategies, has very few classroom discipline problems. As Boykin (1979) has noted, schools need not be "unstimulating, constraining, and monotonous" places where children are usually bored; thus, teachers must channel students' high energy levels into productive, task-oriented activities. Teacher education students receive very little applied training in motivational techniques.

Although human relations classes have been incorporated into many teacher education programs since the early 1970s, in addition to in-service cultural and racial awareness seminars for novice and veteran teachers in school districts, the best way for teachers to learn about their diverse students is through real situations (Goodwin, 1990). Education majors, therefore, must be exposed to a variety of students and schools as early as their first semester of pre-service education. They should be assigned to different schools and classrooms every semester of their four- or five-year programs so that they can both observe and participate in the daily activities of teachers in varied school situations. Moreover, students n methods courses should be required to tutor and to perform micro teaching classrooms and schools so that they can "reality test" the suitability of particular instructional approaches with children of exceptional, average, and below-average abilities.

Teacher education majors, therefore, should be required to have a minimum of twenty hours of combined one-on-one tutoring, group or classroom instruction, and specific methods courses so that they can practice teaching content to students while simultaneously applying varied instructional techniques.

Teacher education programs must also devote more attention to the important roles that the home, parents, and community play in the effective education of children, especially those who come from urban cities and rural communities. Novice teachers must be trained how to communicate better and work more closely with the parents of their students.

Teacher education programs must be restructured to accommodate the diverse teaming and cultural styles of elementary and secondary school populations. This goal cannot be accomplished with one course focusing on multicultural populations, through orientation and in- service seminars, or through a single field experience in an urban or rural school. A

173

holistic approach to teacher training must be developed that recognizes the strengths in diverse student populations rather than placing emphasis on cultural-deficit models to explain low performance by children of particular backgrounds. Teachers must also take into consideration the context of the school and the diversity of their students in planning and organizing instruction and use pedagogical techniques that are most appropriate for the grade and subject matter that is being taught.

Teachers must also learn more about classroom management, and motivational techniques during their pre-service years so that children can develop appropriate social skills and personal confidence, in addition to their academic talents. Teachers must be afforded more opportunities to practice these skills, and in varied settings, through more clinical experiences throughout their undergraduate and graduate training. Finally, students who will teach must learn how to communicate more closely with the parents of their children, to motivate, encourage, and reward children's academic performance.

In conclusion, prospective teachers must be trained to believe that all children, regardless of race and social class, can learn and succeed. All teachers, regardless of their own racial or ethnic backgrounds, must realize the important role they can play in shaping students' career aspirations, their academic and personal expectations. Teacher training institutions must prepare for an American educational system whose population will be thoroughly diverse by the year 2000.

Education leaders must focus research attention on the problems of schools with diverse student population and develop appropriate programs to prepare teachers for these schools. Possible solutions include such techniques as forming dynamic partnerships among universities, public schools, businesses, parent groups, and social service agencies; implementing policies and procedures that ensure racial and cultural fairness; and making bilingual education services readily available.

References

American Association of Colleges for Teacher Education. *(1988). Teacher education pipeline: Schools, colleges, and departments of education enrollments by race and ethnicity.* Washington DC: American Association of Colleges for Teacher Education.

Banks, W.C. McQuater, G.V & Hubbard, J.L. (1979). Toward a reconceptualization of the social-cognitive bases of achievement orientations in blacks. In A. W. Boykin, A. J. Franklin, and J. F. Yates (eds.), *Research directions on black psychologists.* New York: Russell Sage Foundation

Boykin, A. W. (1979). Psychological/behavioral verve: Some theoretical explorations and empirical manifestations. (N A. W. Boykin, A. J. Franklin, and J. F. Yates (eds.), *Research directions of Black Psychologists.* New York: Russell Sage Foundation.

Burstein, N. D & Cabello, B. (1989). Preparing teachers to work with culturally diverse students: A teacher education model. *Journal of Teacher Education:* 40(6), 9-16.

Clark, R. *(1983). Family life and school achievement: "Why black children succeed or fail."* Chicago: University of Chicago Press.

Crisci, P.E & Tutels, A.D. (1990). Preparation of educational administrators for urban settings. *Urban Education:* 24(4). 414-430.

Fleishcher, J. & Van Acker, R. (1990). Changes in the urban school population: Challenges in meeting the need for special education leadership and teacher preparation personnel. Paper presentation: ED 343340.

Garibaldi, AM and Zimpher, N. (1989) *1988 National survey of students in teacher education programs.* Washington, DC: American Association of Colleges for Teacher Education,

Garibaldi, AM *(1992) Preparing teachers for culturally diverse classrooms.* In M. Dilworth, (Ed.), Diversity in Teacher Education: Jossey-Bass, San Francisco, CA.

Holmes Group. NE: Author. (1986). *Tomorrow's teachers: A report of the Holmes Group.* East Lansing, Johnson, D. W., and Johnson, R. T. (1989). *Cooperation and competition: Theory and research.* Edina, UN: Interaction Book.

Liston, D., & Zeichner, K. (1990). Teacher education and the social context of schooling: Issues for curriculum development. *American Educational Research Journal: 2,* 7(4), 611-636.

Marquez Chisholm, I. (1994). Preparing teachers for multicultural classrooms *The Journal of Educational Issues of language Minority students,* 14, 43-67.

National Education Association. (1987). *Status of the American Public school teacher, 1985-86* Washington, DC: National Education Association.

Oakes, J (1985). *Keeping track: How schools structure inequality. New* Haven, CT: Yale University Press.

Rios, F. (1993) Thinking in urban multicultural classrooms:

Four teachers' perspectives. *Urban Education: 28(3),* 245-266.

Rogus, J.F. (1987) The preparation of teachers for urban schools: Creating a crisis. *Metropolitan Education: 4,* 30-40.

Ross, D & Smith, W. (1992) Understanding preservice teachers' perspectives on diversity. *Journal of Teacher Education: 43(2) 94-103.*

Standards for teacher competence in the educational assessment of students. (1989). Washington, DC: American Association of Colleges for Teacher Education, American Federation of Teachers, National Council on Measurement in Education, and National Education Association,

Willis, M. G. (1989). Learning styles of African American children: A review of the literature and interventions. *Journal of Black Psychology: 16, 1.*

Wilson, R. (1988). Recruiting and retaining minority teachers. *The Journal of Negro Education:* 57(2), 195-198.

CHAPTER 15

Headlights in the Night – Using Problem-Based Learning Across the Professional Education Curriculum to See Diverse Students as the Norm

Kathryn Newman, Ph.D.
Grambling State University
Grambling, LA

Statement of the problem

The purpose is to present through a symposium how one teacher education program is using problem-based learning (PBL) and an integrated professional education curriculum delivery system to allow preservice teachers to build one dynamic, inter-connected knowledge base of teaching that crosses not only content areas, but also areas within the field of instruction. The integrated curriculum extends from the classes to the field experiences.

This strategy increases the quality of preservice teachers by requiring them to not only learn about theories, research and practices in teaching, but also to analyze and evaluate them. It also works to increase the number of teachers who are uniquely suited to working with an increasingly diverse student population by giving them the skills to successfully navigate the teacher education program, then take those same skills of problem-based learning and reflection into their classrooms to facilitate critical thinking in their students. One of the most troubling reasons for the discrepancy between low-income and middle income students, and between dominant culture and minority students is the lack of access to a quality education which includes access to qualified teachers who are capable of imparting a sense of excellence to their students. (Darling-Hammond, 1995) It is our position that training preservice teachers to think about their own work in a different way will result in differences in their students' academic achievements. Tharp and Gailimore (1989) have posited, teachers teach in the ways that they were taught- not the ways that they were taught to teach. Teachers must have more complete knowledge bases that allow critical analysis and reflection (Alley & Jung, 1995; Darling-Hammond, 1996; and Ladson-Billings, 1995).

Without changes in how teacher educators approach the concept of building knowledge, teaching cannot move into the 21st century, and certainly cannot produce teachers that promote excellence within their educational spheres. Consequently, they cannot make a difference in the learning of all students. Those

180

students with outside access to educational venues will continue to perform well (see Popham, (1999) for a discussion). Unfortunately, those without access to outside quality education will continue to be discarded, retained in grades, referred to special education, or simply ignored in the classroom.

The theories of what teachers' should know and how they should learn it have not kept up with either policies or trends. With calls for teachers' to become reflective practitioners (e.g. Darling-Hammond, 1996) teacher educators must examine how and what we teach preservice teachers' about the teaching and learning processes. Without re-examination, teachers will remain largely ignorant of not only critical knowledge needed to formulate policies and implement constructivist practices that will help students, but also lack the analytical skills to evaluate this information. In short, teachers' are a summation of their own educational experiences. Thus, if they were educated using rote memorization, convergent thinking, and intellectual suffocation (e.g., one text, with little divergent discussion allowed); they are more likely to use those strategies when teaching their own classes. Therefore, to create change in teaching practices in the schools, teachers must experience educational methods that require reflection and critical analysis, create opportunities for problem solving, and demonstrate planning for diverse groups of learners.

The problem is that the delivery system is still fragmented, and candidates are often unable to assemble the bridges or scaffolds needed to create meaningful associations between knowledge bases. Consequently, a student may be unable to connect how the learning environment that was studied in a previous class or even a textbook would relate to assessment data gathered in the present class, classroom management in the next. From a constructivist approach, the learners have not had ample opportunities to construct working models of the concept (Spivey, 1997). These opportunities should have required active participation, testing, cognitive analysis and reflection in order to construct knowledge that is itself active, dynamic, reflective and self-perpetuating. This problem was particularly observed in two of my classes-- an assessment course required of most education majors, a class in exceptionality, required of early childhood, elementary and special education majors. The preservice teachers often failed to realize that information gathered in earlier or concurrent classes in the areas of test selection, alternative means of assessment, interpretation of data, characteristics of diverse learners, and intensive teaching methods, was directly applicable to other classes. Therefore, part of the goal of using problem-based learning was to teach inquiry, encourage generalization, form cognitive associations (semantic webs) and reawaken creativity.

182

It must be remembered that teaching is not just a series of collected facts. It is as much a science, as an art, as a skill, as a craft. It is also a series of dynamic interactions with 20 to 30 or more separate environments requiring a large block of theoretical and research knowledge, constant monitoring, feedback, and observation. Too often, preservice teachers are unprepared for the fast pace of the average classroom. Furthermore, they are neither used to reflecting, nor being able to change patterns of action in the face of failure. Add to this volatile mixture, an inability to create bridges of commonality between teacher and learners who are often culturally, economically, or linguistically diverse and a recipe for student failure has again been created.

Literacy forms the foundation of the new style being used. In this case, the professional literature is the starting point for the problem-based learning. In this respect, I follow Bloom's Taxonomy in that I believe that a knowledge base must first be firmly established before more complex and analytical associations and evaluations can be made. This knowledge base is determined not only from texts, but also from professional journals, newsletters, newspapers, popular journals and the Internet. These multiple sources for knowledge are important because they can also be examined for not only content, but also for clarity and implications. Often information given in one form is changed for another. Literacy is therefore more than the ability to read and comprehend printed communications. In fact, at the professional level - literacy must also be the ability to evaluate the efficacy of the information given. For instance, preservice teachers are given the task of reading excerpts from the books *The Bell Curve* and *Rage of Privileged Class.* Both excerpts deal with the same incident at the Georgetown University law school. However, the books' treatment of that incident are markedly different, in that critical information given in one, is omitted in the other - thus changing the tone of' the incident. Preservice teachers need to not only be familiar with the theories and methods, but also able to reflect upon the knowledge in order to judge its usefulness. Then once the reflective knowledge base is created, real world problems are posed to test the knowledge gained.

The applicability of problem-based learning

Problem based learning grew out of changes in medical school instruction (Delisle, 1997). Students are viewed as stake-holders then immersed in ill-structured, "messy" problems without easy solutions. Students attempting to "solve" these problems are required to used meta-cognitive steps, identify what they need to know, define variables for further investigation, then propose and test solutions.

Education is a prime area for using problem-based teaming based upon its characteristics. First, the central problem in problem-based learning must be sloppy. In education, very few problems are neat and easily solved. Preservice teachers report through anecdotes that many real problems are not even posed in current textbooks (e.g., case #5 in the appendix). In fact, with PL 105-17, and the mandates for inclusion, many of the traditional lines that were drawn to separate diverse learners are now found to be artificial in that many of the methods used for "one group" from precision teaching to enrichment, simply makes sound educational sense across the curriculum. Second, new information pertaining to the problem often changes the focus. This is similar to the way that airline pilots are trained in simulators before even getting into the actual airliner. Third, there is often no one right answer (case #3). Fourth, it gives the preservice teachers a reason to reach outside of their comfort zone and act as detectives (cases #4 & 6), apply facts to act as advocates (cases #1 & 2), or create networks with other professionals (case #7). In fact, when first presented with case #3, most preservice teachers reflect that they are stunned to learn that this essay was generated by a middle school-aged student neither in special education, nor judged to be in need of specialized services. The secondary majors who had expressed dismay that they had to study the acquisition of reading and writing skills as well as reading and writing at their own level now had to call upon that knowledge in order to outline an intervention for the student. The preservice teachers then see concretely that individualized educational service does not need to be formal to be useful, and that interventions taught in the class for "exceptional students", from enrichment to guided notes, are practiced over multiple ability levels and backgrounds.

Using problem-based learning has produced an unexpected outcome. The preservice teachers seem to delight in using their own field experiences to design problems for their peers. I am discovering that allowing preservice teachers to design problems in collaboration with other colleagues creates opportunities for preservice teachers to see the classroom as a series of dynamic interconnected facets. Consequently, learners have a stronger knowledge base; moreover, they can produce, discuss and analyze critical features of teaching and learning along greater and deeper dimensions. While some preservice teachers exhibit a "fear of the unknown' with practice and insistence, the new resources such as web sites for state departments of education, and professional literature and references such as *Test Critiques, Tests in Print* etc become mainstays of new reflective behaviors for many. Furthermore, preservice teachers begin to view their peers as educational resources. In this way, experiences become paths to answers.

Questions generated from using problem-based learning

While there were the anticipated problems of aligning curriculum, designing problems, and providing feedback to encourage further thinking; there were also unanticipated challenges. Specifically, the task of using problem-based learning took on multiple levels where my own problem based learning centered on how to use it effectively. My own history as a special educator often demanded that I not wait until the student was "ready" given that without direct instruction, the student might never demonstrate readiness. Furthermore, I realized from my own educational experiences in the 1970's that student-centered instruction without some guidelines produced some learning, some new experiences, but failed to prepare us for the traditional and standardized curricula reflected in the ACT, SAT, GRE and other assessments of achievement. In this day of high stakes testing of pupils, and preservice teachers, my ongoing problem was and is *"How to stimulate thinking, encourage cognitive associations and yet guide the problem-based learning experienced by the preservice teachers to the information that they will be expected to know (in the expected format) for their own licensure exams, and classrooms?"*

187

My own problem-based learning has become to explore the two questions of how to get them to fly using professional literacy as their updrafts and how to get me to let go of them.

Selected references

Alley, R. & Jung, B. (1995). Preparing teachers for the 21st century. In O'Hair, M.J & Odell, S (Eds). *Educating teachers for leadership and change*, (pp. 285-301). Thousand Oaks. CA: Corwin Press, Inc.

Barell, J. (1999). *Problem-based learning: An inquiry approach.* Arlington Heights, IL: Skylight Training and Publishing.

Brooks, J.G & Brooks, M.G. (1999). *In search of understanding: The case for constructivist classrooms.* Alexandria, VA: Association for Supervision and Curriculum Development.

Darling-Hammond, L. (1996). The quiet revolution: Rethinking teacher development. *Educational Leadership: 53(6), 4-*10.

Delisle, R. (1997). *How to use problem-based learning in the classroom.* Alexandria, VA: Association for Supervision and Curriculum Development.

Fogarty, R. (1998). *Problem-based learning: A collection of articles.* Arlington Heights, IL: Skylight Training and Publishing.

Ladson-Billings, G. (1995). Multicultural teacher education: Research, practice and policy. In J.E. Banks & C.A. Banks (Eds), *Handbook of research on multicultural education* (747-762). New York: Macmillan Publishing.

Darling-Hammond, L. (1995). Inequality and access to knowledge. In J.E. Banks & C.A.Banks (Eds.). *Handbook of research on multicultural education* (465-484). New York: Macmillan Publishing.

Donmoyer, R. (1996). The concept of a knowledge base. In F.B. Murray (Ed). *The teacher educators' handbook (92-*119). San Francisco: Jossey-Bass.

Holt-Reynolds, D (1995). Preservice teachers and coursework: When is getting it right wrong? O'Hair, M.J & Odell, S (Eds.), *Educating teachers for leadership and change (pp.* 117-137). Thousand Oaks, CA: Corwin Press, Inc.

Popham, W.J. (1999). Why standardized tests don't measure educational quality. *Educational Leadership: 56(6),* 8-16.

Powell, R.R. & Zehm, S. & Garcia, J. (1996). *Field experience: Strategies or exploring diversity in schools.* Englewood Cliffs, NJ: Merrill.

Spivey, N.N. (1997). *7he constructivist metaphor.* San Diego, CA: Academic Press.

Stiggins, R. (1991). Relevant classroom assessment training for teachers. *Educational Measurement: Issues and Practice. (*pp 7 – 12)

Tharp, R.G. & Gallimore, R. (1989). *Rousing minds to life.* New York: Cambridge University Press.

Torp, L & Sage, S. (1998). *Problems as possibilities.* Alexandria, VA: Association for Supervision and Curriculum Development.

Case #1 -- Are there legal concerns here?

Your son Darryl (age 10) has a moderate articulation problem for which he receives individual speech therapy. Additionally, he also has demonstrated a mild reading delay. On national tests, he reads approximately one year below his grade level, and his spelling is two years below grade level. It should be noted however, that in comparison to his peers he is at grade level in reading and only a year below them in spelling. His math achievement is at the national average. Therefore, he is educated in the regular classroom with few needs for modifying his educational environment. You have been paying for a college student to tutor him in reading once a week, and both you and Darryl are pleased with the result.

About a month ago, Darryl got into a fight with two older students (ages 12 and 14) who had been teasing him for the previous weeks about his speech. The teacher reported that when one of the two shoved him to the pavement, Darryl retaliated by punching the student in the mouth and breaking a tooth. Darryl was suspended for three days despite your protestations that the other students were not reprimanded, and that the teachers had not intervened regardless of the fact that they had witnessed the teasing. A week after he returned, Darryl reported that he spent much of the day in a room with a stranger "playing games with words and pictures" and answering questions out of a book. Yesterday, you received a phone call from the school asking you to come in today for a meeting about Darryl being moved to a resource room for severely behaviorally disturbed children for 75% of the day. The school personnel told you that the move had been approved, but that your input would be appreciated. When you responded that you were not sure that you agreed with the move, you were told that unless you agreed, Darryl would be declared ineligible to receive school services for the rest of the year. Therefore, you took off from work to attend the meeting, and found that not only was the move already decided, but the IEP had been written without your input. Darryl's regular education teacher was not there, and when you asked about it, saying that she knew his academic level, you were told that she did not have to be involved in the IEP process. The goals and objectives were all skills that Darryl had mastered two years ago, and the IEP stated that Darryl would not be taking the LEAP or ITBS tests anymore because of his new classification.

Is this legal? What problems would a parent advocate or legal advocate point out? What should be happening, and what court cases or Congressional laws back up your conclusions?

Case #2-- A cause for Advocacy?

You volunteer at a group home for mildly and moderately retarded citizens. The center would like to purchase a nicer 4-5 BR house in a residential neighborhood so that they could really experience living as much on their own in as normal a setting as possible. The problem is that a group of 64 "concerned citizens" in that neighborhood have threatened to rezone the area to prevent more than two unrelated or unmarried adults living in the same house, i.e., to keep the group home from relocating there. You know that the clients involved are quiet, responsible, and no trouble to anyone. What are your options? Who are possible resources to help you solve this problem?

Case #3

EXERCISE -- As a teacher, respond to the following homework submitted for one of your assignments by a secondary student:

> *As I read the article, the observation was that as the child got older his speech wasn't as developed like other children. The toddler could say some words, but the parent and adult couldn't understand what that child was trying to say. But as the child got older the speech develop suppose to have gotten better.*
> *The result of speech delays are with all these factors affecting the rate*

of language acquisition, parent or adult
shouldn't be surprise. If parent or adult
have children who have not responded
much to sounds or tried to imitate
them parent, should check with your
pediatrician. Your child may have a
hearing problem.
My opinion about this article
is very interesting. I've learned a great
deal from this article about factors
I didn't understand about speech delays.
The article wasn't too short nor too long
it was just right.

Case #4

Your major:

Your ideal class would be _____ grade, _____ subject

A student is lethargic in your class. The student volunteers little and participates as little as possible in the group discussions. As a member of smaller group project, the student completes what is required, but little else. The student appears to be missing some basic skills required for that level, or at least doesn't use them without prompting. The student often requests to be excused, but other than that poses no problem behaviorally. The student appears to be average age, height and weight in comparison to his/her group.

Is this a problem for the teacher? Why or why not? Using

the theorists that you have studied earlier, outline possible causes for the behavior, and then for each theorist used, outline a strategy for working with that student.

(NOTE: Do not fall back on the overused phrase "I will work with the student to improve/increase his/her academic skills..." That phrase, unless it's accompanied by a clear action plan, means nothing.)

Problem based learning #5

As a new teacher, you have inherited- a class in midyear. The district is considered economically disadvantaged, with less than 70% of the teachers being certified to teach in their assigned areas. This class has had substitutes teachers from the first day, and you find that the class (7th grade- English) *appears* to be behind where the *other* classes are. The parents are protesting the competency testing that is to be conducted in March. Specifically, they are stating that the test selected is biased and that the court system will have to let their children advance. You are asked to prepare a series of written responses. First, evaluate the likelihood that the students in the other classes will do well on the competency test and discuss why. Second, explain to the parents how the courts have ruled in minimum competency test cases. Finally, third, map out a strategy for maximizing the time that you have with the students to increase their chances.

Case #6

A student comes to you with the following information and scores in her cumulative record. All scores were obtained at the end of the school year:

Kdgn.	reading readiness score	$z = +2.00$
	math readiness score	$t = 75$
	language arts attendance	70th percentile
	attendance	missed 26 days this year
1st grade	reading	$t = 62$
	math	$t = 72$
	language arts	$z = +.89$
	social studies	50th percentile
	attendance	missed 35 days this year
2nd grade	reading	22nd percentile
	math	$z = -1.27$
	science	1st percentile
	language arts	$t = 37$
	attendance	missed 56 days due to hospitalization (heart surgery); allowed to advance because of visiting teacher

3rd grade	reading	grade equiv. =1.9
	math	$t = 27$
	social studies	1st percentile
	science	1st percentile
	language arts	grade equiv. = 1.5
	recommendations	evaluation for special education

You are a 4th grade teacher who may get this student. What happened to this student? Where did the breakdown occur? Why might special education *not* be the best option? What would you suggest in its place? Create your answer in the form of a report to either a parent or an administrator.

Problem based learning #7

Your major:
Your ideal class would be _____ grade, _____subject

Your school's faculty needs to do extensive revision of the way that they deliver the information. The teachers' committee decides that all subject areas need to focus on *Reading Comprehension Skills, Vocabulary, and Decoding Skills* in order to improve your students' scores on the yearly standardized test, as well as the yearly High School Exit Exams.

First, go to the Louisiana State Department of Education's web site, and looking under "Foundation Skills" decide whether your schools plan to focus on these skills in reading may improve test scores and discuss your decision. If you decide that your school's plan is a poor one, *or you can improve on it,* present an alternative and explain why that plan should be used.

Second, discuss how you would rearrange your class to reflect either the plan presented, or your own plan. How would you design the *environment* (both the physical environment, and the teaching climate) to reflect the new emphasis? Be sure to cite at least three sources of research and theories that pertain to the learning climate.

(NOTE: for extra credit (up to 5 points if well done), complete this assignment by starting with the web site of a *different* state! See what others are doing!)

CHAPTER 16

Literacy for Life Success:
Using Critical Pedagogy in Developmental and Educational
Psychology

Nanthalia W. McJamerson, Ph.D.
Wasika Goodie, Preservice Teacher
Grambling State University
Grambling, LA

Sandra F. Thomas
Tunir Mutakabbir
South Carolina State University

Second class literacy is rampant in some communities. According to critical pedagogical advocates, this problem "calls for a move towards literacy models which highlight the importance of social and cultural contexts that allow for reading the word and the world" (Freire & Macedo, 1987).

After studying the critical pedagogy, such as Paulo Freire's (1973) *Pedagogy of the Oppressed*, Henry Giroux's (1978, 1992) *Pedagogy of the Immaculate Perception*, Harold and Ann Berlak's *Dilemma Language of Schooling* (1981) and Ira Shor's (1987) *Reconstructed Learning Approach*, a project titled *"Reconstructing Lives"* was created as a critical literacy approach for taking the mystery out of success (McJamerson, N., 1998). The project has been used in the training of teachers and counselors, with an emphasis on student achievement.

The work of demystifying success through the "RECONSTRUCTING" Lives Project began in 1991 as four graduate counseling majors at South Carolina State University diligently searched for those factors which transformed persons who faced extraordinary obstacles into persons with extraordinary achievements in their lives. Their worked produced a "Success Fibers Model of Development" based on their discovery of six essential factors or common fibers in the lives of achievers: (1) Ability Nurture, (2) Ambition Ignition, (3) Cardiac Reserve, (4) Competency Training, (5) Opportunity Ramrods and (6) Insight Dividends (McJamerson, N., 1998).

Two assumptions underpin the project. First, if we develop a deeper understanding of the multiple interactions and intricate transactions among factors which lead to success, we can then increase the possibilities for successful lives. Second, if we study success (Wolin & Wolin, 1994) as intensely as we study failure, then we will be able to unleash the "arrested development" (Akbar, 1994) and "unbank the fire" (Hale, 1995) in people's lives.

Several versions of the project have been implemented. In each case the results are positive. On the survey used to determine the impact of the "Reconstructing" Lives Project, participants reported the development of a sense of empowerment in four categories: (1) increased insight; (2) increased encouragement; (3) new awareness of possibilities for personal success and (4) actual behavior changes and plans for behavior changes to create personal success (McJamerson, N., 1998).

Observations indicated that project participants discovered and discussed similarities between their own struggles and strengths and those of successful persons, and they, subsequently, analyzed their own behavior regarding success. Furthermore, rather than merely admire or stand in awe of famous persons, participants expressed the possibilities of creating transformations in their own lives (McJamerson, N., 1998).

In the present chapter, three examples will be presented to demonstrate the empowerment, which resulted from the simultaneous development of literacy skills, critical thinking and action plans for personal and professional success.

Case 1: Studying the Life of Dr. Ben Carson
Studied by Sandra F. Thomas
Ben Carson had quite a story to tell. When I started the book, I would only put it down to go asleep. I enjoyed every page of the book. His story has made a major impact on my life. I have

always been a highly motivated person, but now I feel that I have more energy. It has always been my philosophy that I can do anything I set out to do and I actually believe that. This book has enriched my life. I will never see life the same again. Words cannot express the joy I felt when I saw that Ben Carson did not forget his foundation--- his mother. Thank you for selecting this book as an assignment. This book should be read by students, parents, administrators, and teachers everywhere.

Ben Carson had so many people that made a difference in his life. I can only choose four (4) for the sake of this project. Therefore, I would say that key persons in Ben Carson's life were Sonya Carson, Pastor Ford, Mrs. Williamson, and Curtis Carson Sonya Carson played a very important role in her son's life. She was hard working, goal oriented, driven to demand the best of herself in any situation. She refused to settle for less. Her most outstanding characteristic was that she had a natural ability, an intuitive sense that enabled her to perceive what had to be done. She did not allow Ben to settle for less than the best he could do. Because of her constant encouragement, Ben and his brother, Curtis, believed they could do anything they chose to do. During his life, I am sure that Ben could still hear her voice saying "Bennie, you can do it. Don't you stop believing that for one

202

second,". Although his mother only had a third grade education, she still provided the driving force in their home.

Sonya Carson had to be a remarkable woman. Although she made many visits to the mental institution, this woman still had a lot of strength. Her inner strength helped her realize she needed professional help. She was away from her children for periods of time. But she always left them with someone she felt comfortable with. This lady was focused on having her sons make something of themselves and she did a remarkable job. She always made time for her boys, no matter how tired she was and she always asked them about school.

Dr. Carson's crediting of his mother has moved me. I am happy to know that according to his success story, I am on the right track with my children. I do not believe in wasting a whole lot of time on TV and I push my children to excel and to do their best. My daughter had a bad experience with her math grades for one year. It was such a shock for me because from K-5th grade she was an honor roll student. Despite what people might say, a lot of teachers are not doing a good job with their students. But when problems like this occur it is our responsibility to see that our children get back on the right track. Thank God, we made it through that year and my daughter is back on the honor roll.

Pastor Ford told of a missionary doctor and his wife who were chased by robbers in a far-off country. He told how they dodged around trees and rocks, always keeping ahead of the bandits. Suddenly they were trapped. Then right at the edge of the cliff, they saw a small break in the rock- a split just big enough for them to crawl into and hide. When the men came back, they could not find the doctor and his wife. Then the Pastor looked over the congregation. He told of how the couple was protected and how they were hidden in the cleft of the rock, and God protected them from harm.

Although, Ben was only eight years of age, this story followed him throughout his life. Ben's imagination focused on how God took care of those people and he believed he would take care of him, too. He and his brother joined the church and were baptized a few weeks later. Ben knew he needed God's help if he was going to become a missionary doctor.

"That's what I want to do," he said to his mother as they walked home. "I want to be a doctor.

Can I be a doctor, Mother? "Bennie," she said. "Listen to me." They stopped walking and his mother stared into his eyes. Then, laying her hand on Ben's shoulders, she said, "If you ask the Lord for something and believe He will do it, then, it'll happen." She really had faith in God and she believed in her sons.

Mrs. Williamson *evidently was born to be a teacher. She was always encouraged Ben. It is important for teachers to see whatever potential a student has and try to make them achieve their best. What a teacher says to a student can be devastating. I admire Mrs. Williamson for the position she took with Ben. She never gave up on him. That's what I like about her. She saw improvement in Ben. The small talks that she and Ben had together meant so much to him. She pulled him to the side and said, "on the whole you're doing better, so much better." This teacher was talking about a student who was making F's in math, now making a D. To most teachers, this grade would still be failure, but Mrs. Williamson along with his devoted mother gave him hope.*

Ben's brother, Curtis, was also a good role model for him. Curtis always looked out for his brother. I admire the way he took such an interest in what his brother liked. When he saw that Ben was interested in psychology, he sacrificed to buy Psychology Today *for his brother. Curtis was sensitive to his brother's needs.*

Curtis was the main reason that Ben joined the ROTC. Ben really admired his brother. Ben never told Curtis how much he admired him or what a positive role model he was to him. Ben was proud of his brother's medals and ribbons.

When Ben joined the ROTC, his life was changed. He earned several medals and ribbons. In fact, he made it all the way to Colonel, even though he joined the ROTC late.

There are so many programs that would have benefited Ben. It would have been wonderful if he had had a mentor, a good guidance counselor, positive role models (especially Blacks in the medical field), the Big Brothers Organization, and the Boy Scouts.

If you would remove Mrs. Williamson from Ben's life, I do not believe he would have had the confidence in himself that he did. Although his mother was pushing him, he was with that teacher more than he was with her. Parents fail to realize that our children are with the teacher for at least eight (8) hours out of the day. We as parents need the cooperation from the teachers as well as their support to encourage our children. Mrs. Williamson never gave up on Ben. As I previously stated, I believe she was born to be a teacher.

I believe that if Ben had not gotten all of the encouragement from Mrs. Williamson, he would have struggled throughout school making "F's" and possibly "D's." However, he still probably would have had the encouragement about his academics from his mother. Mrs. Williamson made a drastic difference in his life. I doubt if he would have even pursued the medical field had it not been for her. Because of his mother's and

206

brother's support, I still believe he would have had a good job making a descent living. Mrs. Carson would not have stood for anything less for her boys.

Case 2: Studying the Life of Dr. Ben Carson
Studied by Tamir Mutakabbir

As I completed my reading of the Ben Carson story, there were factors that "leaped off" the pages at me. However, I think there are some subtle and hidden factors that are just as powerful as or even more powerful than the obvious factors that propelled Ben Carson to success.

The first and most obvious success factor is Sonya Carson who possessed drive, determination, courage, and vision on her mission to help her sons obtain a formal education. When I think of Ben Carson's mother, I think of the man who approached that prophet with a seemingly simple question: "Who should be the most important person in my life?" The prophet answered, "Your mother." Paradise for Ben Carson was with his mother because, for all of us, mother is our first teacher.

Like Ben Carson, I have an older brother and it is a very good thing to have a brother to pave the way for you. I thought it was very special when my brother would outgrow a toy and give it

207

to me. I usually had wanted it anyway. The foregoing makes it easy for me to be empathetic toward Ben receiving a subscription to Psychology Today from Curtis, his brother. Curtis set a very good example for Ben, and I think Curtis was also a major factor that also helped to propel Ben to success. I believe Ben's road to success was made all the more smooth by Curtis because he was someone that Ben could talk to who would understand certain problems.

The third factor that I believed played a major role in Ben Carson's success was the ROTC. In the ROTC, Ben learned several very important principles. First, he learned how to come from a deficit all the way to the top position for which he yearned. Even after starting a half semester late in the ROTC program, he was able to become the student leader of the unit. He learned some very important leadership skills that will last him a lifetime.

The fourth and final factor that I would like to discuss in this report is what I call the "zeitgeist". This term is defined as the moral and intellectual spirit of the times. What we must understand is that if the times are not right, there is no amount of training, mothers' love, money, talent, nor even "gifted hands" or influential friendships that can make success happen as it has for Ben Carson. "Excuse me boy, would you get my bags for me?" The preceding statement was made by an elderly European-

American female, recently in a major metropolitan airport. She was addressing an African-American male who was an airline pilot. His reply to her was, "I flew the plane into this airport, ma'am; isn't that enough?" The legendary journalist, Carl Rowan was mowing his lawn one day when a European-American male walked up and asked, "How much are you charging to cut these folks' lawn, boy?" Mr. Rowan said, "Well sir, the lady here lets me sleep with her." I cite the above examples to point out to the reader that if the times are not right, then it would be virtually impossible to reach your fullest human potential. George Washington Carver was one of the greatest scientists who ever lived, yet because of the "zeitgeist" in which he lived, I do not believe that he ever reached his fullest human potential. Earnest Everett Just, one of the founders of Omega Psi Phi Fraternity and a pioneering scientist, with his work on the zygote, is another African- American who worked miracles with little or no equipment but could not reach his fullest potential because of the "spirit of the times."

The immediate and personal side of Carson was very beautifully portrayed in the autobiography. Many lessons can be taken from his story and even though his mother is not perfect, she certainly has qualities that should be emulated by the mothers of the world. Ben illustrates a healthy image of an achiever, after he got on the right track.

I sometimes visualize the whole African consciousness as one person and I wonder how this person is functioning. Is this person normal, psychotic, or neurotic? I am convinced that this person is special and has the very best of the essence that humanity deposited within him and her. Ben Carson came from that essence and we need a thousand more like him, for we have them in abundance! We must take the time to refocus on our true selves so that we can cultivate our "Carsons" like Sonya did.

From a symbolic perspective, I look at Ben Carson as once being an ugly old grub worm, moving around on the earth on its stomach and crawling through garbage and all sorts of mess-what a lowly existence. But, this little worm crawls into the cocoon of its mother's existence and begins to take form. With the help of Sonya Carson, Curtis Carson, the ROTC experience and numerous other factors, Ben Carson emerges as a "beautiful butterfly" that has found his calling in life. He knows what he wants to do for the rest of his life and this has to be a sort of self-actualization, at least professionally.

Even though many African-Americans are not able to attain fulfillment in the present age, I believe that because of the work of people like Dr. Martin Luther King, El-Hajj Malik El Shabazz, and others, a zeitgeist was born from which Ben Carson was able to benefit. If this "spirit of the times" did not exist, Ben Carson may have just been a general practitioner trying to help his people survive, for at best he would have only been able to serve African-Americans. So, I will call this factor the "zeitgeist factor", for I believe that if one can come along at the right time, he or she can maximize and reach their fullest human potential.

Case 3: Studying the Life of Patrice Gaines
Studied by Wasika Goodie

Studying the life of Patrice Gaines taught me something about my present behavior or experiences and about my future goals. There are factors to look for, fight for, work for, or get help with in order to reach my goals. The lessons I learned from this person's life are explained below.

The first lesson I learned is to always love and respect myself first. Reading this touching story has made me realize the importance of loving myself. I know that I can't love anyone else if I do not first love myself. In order to do that, I must search within to find peace and acceptance in my life. Once I have found that, then I can begin searching for the love of self that everyone should have. If I spend my days catering to a man, then I don't love myself. If I am too much of a coward to stand up and say "no" to

211

someone, then I can't love myself. I must be able to took at my life and be honest about what I see. If I lie to myself, then I will never be able to change my life for the better. Change can only occur when I am able to admit that something is wrong.

Respect will follow change because if I can admit that there is a problem. Then, I can respect myself for admitting to it. Once I have found that wellspring of love and respect within, then I can share it with the world. This way, everyone can benefit from my newfound happiness. First, I must get right with God and myself before I go out helping people find the love within themselves.

Studying the life of Patrice Gaines taught me a second lesson: if I believe in myself, anything is possible. Patrice Gaines was a woman who didn't believe in herself. She thought that she had to be popular in order to be somebody. She didn't realize that being a black woman made her unique. As long as she had the approval of someone, she felt that her life had meaning. In contrast, I don't need to "belong" in order to feel good about myself I know that I have a tremendous amount of power because I am a black woman. Encouragement from other people is an important part of my self-esteem, but I have developed an unshakable belief in myself. I have always been a very intelligent student- in elementary and junior high school; however, this was not a "good" thing. I was constantly criticized for getting good

212

grades. *My peers called me "teacher's pet" and "goody two-shoes" but I never let that deter me. I knew that in the long run, those good grades would take me farther than being popular ever could. As long as I had good grades, I knew that I could attend any college I wanted and could major in anything I wanted to. I believed that I could make good grades throughout my school years, and I always have. My parents helped a great deal because they pushed me to do my best. Once I got in the habit of doing my best, it became second nature to me. I never tell myself that I can't do something, because I believe otherwise. I know that I can have the world at my feet if I believe that I can do it. There is a song that Whitney Houston and Mariah Carey sing together named "When You Believe". The chorus of this song expresses what I feel about myself:*

> "There can be miracles, when you believe.
> Though hope is frail, it's hard to kill,
> Who knows what miracles you can achieve.
> When you believe, somehow you will.
> You will when you believe."

Lesson three from the study of Patrice Gaines' life is to always keep my eyes open because I never know where a lesson will come from. Just as Patrice Gaines found peace, so must I. When she began working at the Washington Post, she never imagined that she would become close friends with homosexual

213

men. She never closed her heart to them, but rather opened it and learned a great deal from them.

When I first arrived at Grambling State University, I was a shy girl who did not know how to talk to people. I was still trying to "find myself" and I hadn't succeeded yet. There was something inside me that was begging to come out but could not because I didn't know what it was. I was closing myself off to the message my mind was sending. It wasn't until the Spring 1998 semester that I found what I was looking for. NO, it wasn't a man. It was something even better: friends. I've always had the ability to make friends with males faster and easier than with females. So, even after two years, I had only a handful of female friends, if I could even call them that. They were not friends in the truest sense of the word. I could go somewhere with them, but I could not tell them my deepest, darkest secrets. We never had any real conversations about life, love, happiness, or even men.

All that changed-, however, when I met Adriane, Felecia, and Sheree. Finally what was yearning to emerge from within came bursting out. I could sit down and have intellectually stimulating conversations with these women for hours at a time. Once, we took a three-hour trip and never turned on the radio. We didn't need to because we talked for the entire three hours. We don't just gossip, we analyze ourselves and each other. We have so

214

many things in common, that it's scary. We can finish each others'
sentences, we know what the others are thinking, and we
sometimes all say the same thing at the same time. These are
friends in every way, shape, form, and fashion. We have learned
so much from each other.

I could have been like so many other females and figured
that we couldn't be friends because there would always be the
possibility that we would like the same guy. However, I saw them
for what they were, a gift from God. Like Patti LaBelle says,
"Don't Block the Blessings."

In conclusion, reading about the life of Patrice Gaines has
taught me to love and respect myself, believe in myself, and to keep
my eyes open because a lesson can come any unexpected source.

Literacy for Life Success

The positive lessons noted by the writers above as well as the
results of prior implementation of the Reconstructing Lives Project
indicate that literature in the form of autobiographies can be a
powerful tool, not only in increasing literacy activity but also in
promoting higher level thinking and in motivating high
achievement.

REFERENCES

Akbar., N. (1995). Natural psychology and human transformation. Tallahassee, FL: Mind Productions and Associates.

Berlak, A., & Berlak, H. (1981). The dilemmas of schooling. London: Methuen.

Beyer, L.E. (1979). Schools, asthetic forms, and social reproduction. Madison: University of Wisconsin.

Carson, B., & Murphey, C. (1990). Gifted hands. Grand Rapids, MI: Zondervan.

Freire, P. (1973). Pedagogy of the Oppressed. New York: Seabury.

Giroux, H. A. (1992). Literacy, pedagogy, and the politics of difference. Journal of Critical Pedagogy, 19(1).

Giroux, H. A. (1978). Writing and critical thinking in the social studies. Curriculum Inquiry, 8(1), 291-310.

Glaser, B., & Strauss, A. (1976). The discovery of grounded strategies for qualitative research. Chicago: Aldine.

Hale, J. (1994). Unbank the fire: Visions for the education of African-American children. Baltimore: The Johns Hopkins University Press.

McJamerson, N. W. (1998). Reconstructing lives: A reading-for-empowerment project. In Interdisciplinary approaches to issues and practices in teacher education, edited by G. M. Duhon-Boudreaux. Lewiston, NY: The Edwin Mellen Press.

Shor, I. (1992). Empowering education: Critical Teaching for Social Change. Chicago: University of Chicago Press.

Wirth, A. (1983). Productive work in the industry and schools: Becoming persons again. New York: University Press of America.

Wolin, S. J., & Wolin, S. (1993). The resilient self: How survivors of troubled families rise above adversity. New York: Villard Books.

CHAPTER 17

Enlarging the Literacy Bank
Through the Transfer of Study Skills

Christine Paige
Grambling State University
Grambling, LA

Study skills are powerful tools for knowledge acquisition. According to developmental educators, they are especially important for maximizing "second chances" at academic growth. Are study skills transferable? The response to this question is dependent upon particular factors and conditions, which must be put in place in order for study skills to be instructionally transferable. First, the transfer of study skills must be an explicit goal of instruction. Second, the learning environment should have a climate of guided and meaningful teaming strategies. Finally, learning is incomplete until it has been put to use; therefore, application is important.

Transfer of study skills is the focus of this chapter, as study skills are critical determinants of school success (Holschuh & Nist, 1999). Transfer of learning from one situation to another occurs when the learner perceives that two situations contain similar elements and operate in like fashion, A common example is that students who are able to find a word in the dictionary should be able to locate a subject in an encyclopedia. The two situations are not identical, but they do contain similar elements.

The facilitation of transfer is an outgrowth of learning with meaning and is likely to develop in a classroom where the teacher has created a climate of guided and meaningful learning. Teaching, however, increases the certainty that transfer will occur. Students who are given practice in applying what they have learned in one field to other- fields of learning, who are urged to generalize as they work with details and who are required to seek out aspects of present situations that are relative elsewhere are certain to perform better than students who do not have the benefits of such teaching. By asking students what they perceive their needs to be and how they rank those needs in terms of their importance, more effective and meaningful study skills services can be rendered.

Many students encounter transfer of learning problems when they attend seminars, workshops, or orientation sessions that include instruction in study strategies. The study strategies taught are generalized in an attempt to make them more appropriate for the "typical" college class. However, students often do not transfer from the general instruction to their specific course work (Sheets &

220

Rings, 1980). According to Thomas and Moorman (1983), students often lack refined study skills because the transfer of these skills to actual learning tasks was never taught. In addition, Christen & Searfoss (1986) state that teaching study skills in a separate course or program do not result in their transfer to specific content; therefore, they advocate infusing courses with the direct instruction of applicable study skills.

Nist and Simpson (1987), two instructors in the Developmental Studies Reading Program at the University of Georgia, conducted a five-year study that focused on student application of reading skills to regular college courses. They developed a hypothesis that would avoid or correct this situation. These teachers-researchers experimented with a content-based program that emphasized three strategies that were believed to promote self-regulated learning and transfer. The experiment proved to be successful because the three strategies or processes are still being used. The three processes are planning, monitoring, and evaluating (Brown, 1982). Students in the program have SAT scores of 790 and predicted college averages of 1.7. Students are described as lacking the ability to comprehend lengthy textbooks and having little or no metacognition skills.

During the first four weeks, students were taught active reading of college tests and preparation for objective, and essay exams. Specifically, they learned underlining, annotating, mapping, predicting test questions, and a number of rehearsal self-questioning, and fix-up strategies. For the remainder of the ten-week sessions, students are prepared for four content area tests. Namely, they learn how to select appropriate strategies, make study plans, and apply the strategies to textbook chapters. Students must earn a grade of "B" or above on the four exams. Any student who does not meet these requirements must enroll for another ten-week session. These students are not allowed to take courses in the regular curriculum.

Research data indicates that long-term student success is a result of this approach to college reading. This content approach helps students to become independent learners. Reports show that students who have successfully completed this content reading course are successful in regular college course work. The strategy of using testimonials, feedback, and discussions about successes and frustrations is a point of positive reaction and agreement. This strategy is found to simulate interest and motivation. The development of study plans creates pride and self-evaluation. Other positive features of this model result from the self-evaluation process, which enables students to objectively make decisions to improve inefficient study habits.

References

Crew, A. (1987). "A rationale for experiential education." Contemporary Education, 58(3).

Cross, K. P. (1976). Accent on learning. San Francisco: Jossey-Bass.

Hittleman, D. (1978). Developmental reading. Chicago: Rand McNally College Publishing Company.

Karlin, R. (1974). Teaching reading in high school. New York: Bobbs-Merrill.

Nist, S., & Simpson, M. (1987). Journal of Reading, 30(7).

Roueche, J. E., & Snow, J. J. (1977). Overcoming Learning Problems. San Francisco: Jossey-Bass.

Sheets, R., & Rings, S. (1989). "Ideas in practice: Tailor-Made study strategies: A success story!" Journal of Developmental Education, 12(3).

Thomas, K., & Moorman, G. (1983). Designing reading programs. Dubuque, IA: Kendall/Hunt.

CHAPTER 18

Mind Development, Inc.: Teacher Expectations and Student Achievement

Gail Lee, M. Ed.
Grambling State University
Grambling, LA

Often, educators reserve their high expectations and high quality schooling experiences for students who are labeled as advanced or gifted. Researchers have shown us for decades the detrimental effects of teachers' low expectations on "low or average" students (Rosenthal, 1992). The author of this chapter believes in the ability of all students and designed a creative framework, Mind Development, Inc., which demands the best from her students.

According to the educational literature, a teacher's expectations can have a strong influence upon students' academic achievement. The work of Rosenthal and Jacobson (1992), and others, has shown what is known as the "self-fulfilling prophecy". As an educator in the college developmental program, I have seen the need for positive teacher expectations, as well as a need for guidance in the learning process. On that basis, and my personal teaching philosophy, I created the Mind Development, Inc. concept. Positive results have come from this concept. This teacher has received scores of appreciation letters and visits from students who became successful after leaving college, and they specifically cited the teaching approach. In this chapter, major components of the Mind Development, Inc. are presented.

Company Philosophy

The focus of our study of communication will be targeted to but not limited to the aspects of <u>written</u> communication.

The premise of written communication is dependent upon two important factors:

- understanding the theoretical principles underlying effective communication behavior
- practical application of those principles in various written exercises

Company Theory

For the purpose of our study in English 092, and English 093, the written word will be the primary tool of communication and composition. Just as the journey of a thousand miles begins with one single step, the road to mastering the written composition begins with the control of its smallest unit, the word.

All words can be classified into one of eight categories of speech. A word is a concept, a combination of sounds which forms an independent unit of thought. Since all writing and speaking consists of concepts, it is correct to say that our ideas are no better than our vocabularies, i.e., our word supplies.

The first approach to writing is self-evaluation. The whole process of writing consists of two fundamental steps: first, finding out what we think and feel about people, places, happenings, and ideas; and second, communicating those thoughts and feelings to our readers. The first step requires thinking and the second one requires writing.

A common sense approach to the problem of essay writing entails individualized treatment. In essence, the most interesting and effective subjects for themes are those about which we either have some knowledge of or genuinely want to learn something about Therefore, writing is created by the ideas and impressions, which we have obtained from various sources. Naturally, we get much of our material from our own experiences, observation curiosity, imagination, and reflections. Therefore, you cannot avoid writing about yourself or revealing yourself in many ways.

As you write, there will be certain revelations revealed

about <u>YOU,</u> the writer. These revelations are called elements of style, i.e., a writer's way of expressing himself Therefore; your own "winning style" must begin with ideas in your head. As you begin thinking of ways to reveal your thoughts and feelings, be sure to take time to think about your audience. To be certain that what you write will be both communicable and interesting, always consider your READERS!

Last but not least students of both English 092 and 093 will learn the effective and correct use of marks of punctuation. One of the most important tools for making paper "speak" in your own voice is punctuation. When speaking aloud, you punctuate constantly--body language. Your listener "hears" commas, dashes, question marks, exclamation points and quotation marks as you shout, whisper, pause, wave your arms, roll your eyes or wrinkle your brow.

In writing, punctuation plays the role of body language. It helps the reader "hear" the way you want to be heard. There are thirty (30) main punctuation marks, however you will need approximately about a dozen for most writing. It is this group that we shall direct our attentions toward. As hard-working employees (students), you will learn to master the actual mechanics of writing. These include:

- Where To Begin,
- How to Write Clearly,
- How To Write With Style, and
- How To Punctuate.

Company Procedures

This company has as its main resource the "power" of the written word. For the students/employees in <u>English 092,</u> we will cover an in-depth study of words as they relate to grammatically correct and logically constructed sentences. Words are classified according to their use in larger units of thought, that is, sentences. Therefore, it is not easy to phrase good sentences without an understanding of grammatical terms.

For the students/employees in <u>English 093,</u> the concentration will be on learning and applying the principles of good essay writing. You will be expected to master the principles and concepts used in writing paragraphs that are clear, coherent and unified.

The paragraph is defined as a group of related sentences about one main topic, idea or thought. A paragraph should have enough detail to explain, support or round out the main topic. There are certain unique key elements that should characterize every paragraph. They include UNITY, COHERENCE AND CLARITY!

After you have chosen the idea to be discussed and identified the controlling idea (topic sentence), the next step will be the development of that idea into a well-organized paragraph. There are eight (8) numerous ways of development. However, for the purpose of our study, we will examine forms of basic paragraph development.

The pattern of a paragraph like the pattern of an entire essay reflects the way the writer thinks. These patterns suggest the in-depth questions used to develop a topic. Of course, some paragraphs, like some essays, have more than one pattern of development. As a beginning writer, however, it is advised that you learn to use each pattern separately. Once you have developed good paragraph skills, then you can begin to combine strategies to express your ideas.

Company Guidelines of Documentation

1. The "A" paragraph/essay should possess logic, unity, originality, forceful language, and clarity. The central theme must be evident. It must be supported and developed. The written document should not have fragments, fused sentences, comma splices, or violations of

subject-verb or pronoun-antecedent agreement. There should be commas after introductory adverb clauses and introductory modifying phrases.

2.   The "B" paragraph/essay should have a central theme, which is stated and which is logically developed. The paragraph should be one of originality. The paragraph should not have fragments, fused sentences, comma splices, or violations of subject-verb sentences or pronoun antecedent agreement. There should be no more than three errors in spelling, punctuation or capitalization.

3.   The "C" paragraph/essay may have one of these errors: fragment, fused sentence, comma splice, subject-verb, or pronoun-antecedent violation. The paragraph may have several minor errors. However, these errors will not restrict the clarity of the paragraph to any great extent. The paragraph will not be as creative or as imaginative as the "A" or "B" paragraph.

4.   The "D" paragraph/essay will have two or more major errors. These errors will restrict the clarity and coherence of the paragraph/essay.

5.   The "F" paragraph/essay will have two or more major errors, but it will not have a central theme, unity, clarity, or legal development.

Employee/School Success Factors

Directions: Review each factor and share your feelings about how each factor applies to you as a productive vs. non-productive student. <u>Be honest with yourself.</u>

*NOTE: <u>It is important that you read each factor, do not skip.</u>

<u>Success Factors</u>

1. Studies on a regular basis.
2. Attends class, unless there is an emergency.
3. Manages time well
4. Gets enough rest.
5. Assumes responsibility for <u>own</u> actions (right or wrong).
6. Able to concentrate and focus attention.
7. Takes good notes.
8. Willing to change--is open to changes in the environment and self.
9. Able to suspend judgment--has opinions and positions, but is able to let go of them when appropriate. Doesn't let judgment get in the way of learning.
10. Self-questioning--willing to evaluate self and behavior.
11. Willing to risk--willing to participate in class dialogues at the risk of looking foolish.

232

12. Self-directed--doesn't need others to provide rewards or punishment; has <u>inner</u> motivation.

13. Willing to laugh--ability to laugh at oneself.

14. Hungry--hungry for knowledge.

15. Willing to work--willing to follow through on assignments with sweat. Recognizes the importance of persistence and work.

References

Babab, E., Bernieri, F., & Rosenthal, R. (1991). Students as judges of teachers' verbal and nonverbal behavior. American Educational Research Journal, 28(1), 211-234.

Beez, W. V. (1970). Influence of biased psychological reports on teacher behavior and pupil performance. In M. W. Miles & W. W. Charters, Jr. Learning in Social Settings, Boston: Allyn and Bacon

Brophy, J. (1986). Teacher influences on student achievement, Special Issues: Psychological science and education. American Psychologist, 41(10), 1069-1077.

Brophy, J. (1988). Teacher influences on student achievement: Potential implications for instruction of Chapter I students. Educational Psychologist, 23(3), 235-286.

Brophy, J., & Good, T. L. (1970). Teachers communication of differential expectations for children's classroom performance: Some behavioral data. Journal of Educational Psychology, 61, 365-374.

CHAPTER 19

Preparing Preservice Teachers to Effectively Address Literacy Through Clinical Experiences

Florence Simon
Grambling State University
Grambling, LA

Clinical experience is a process in which an individual develops insights regarding teaching. These experiences are divided into three phases: observation, preservice, and student teaching. Preservice teaching and student teaching are similar. Both preservice teaching and student teaching allow the actual teaching experience to take place. Another benefit of clinical experience is gaining insight relative to the various teaching methods and styles of learning used in the classrooms that foster students to learn what is being taught. In addition to clinical exposure to various teaching methods and styles of learning, clinical experience introduces all phases of teaching groups of preservice teachers. The classrooms of today are composed of diverse groups of children. Children from all over the world and from difference walks of life come together in classrooms. Teacher skills and attitudes influence everything that happens in classrooms. Children view teachers as the most important people in their lives.

Teachers influence children's lives through various means. Teachers who are patient, trustworthy, attentive, and possess a love for learning can more readily pass these qualities to children. Grambling State University's teacher education program is a quality program, which provides preservice teachers with a wide variety of early clinical experiences in a variety of education settings. These experiences formulate a foundation for training education majors. Just as in other fields of study, it is important for education majors to have clinical experiences to strengthen their abilities in the field of education.

John Dewey was a pioneer in the field of learner-centered instruction. He was a strong advocate for the experiential training of teachers. Dewey viewed teachers as learners. In accord with Dewey's vision for teacher preparation, professionals in Teacher Education Department at GSU also believe that student teaching alone is not enough for preservice teachers to experience teaching realistically. Preservice teachers at GSU are required to complete observation/participation hours as part of their teacher training. However, it is believed that education majors should experience the real world of teaching and learning in addition to merely observing.

In interviews conducted with administrators and master teachers across the state of Louisiana, many of them confided that they were having problems with many first-year teachers. The administrators and master teachers discovered that the first-year teachers were skilled in educational theory, but lacked the ability to apply those theories adequately. It was also noted that the beginning teachers were having difficulty meeting the expectations of the administrators and master teachers interviewed.

In an effort to address these concerns and enhance teacher preparation, preservice teachers at GSU are exposed to the components of lesson planning and to the qualities to children. Grambling State University's teacher education program is a quality program, which provides preservice teachers with a wide variety of early clinical experiences in a variety of education settings. These experiences formulate a foundation for training education majors. Just as in other fields of study, it is important for education majors to have clinical experiences to strengthen their abilities in the field of education.

John Dewey was a pioneer in the field of learner-centered instruction. He was a strong advocate for the experiential training of teachers. Dewey viewed teachers as learners. In accord with Dewey's vision for teacher preparation, professionals in Teacher Education Department at GSU also believe that student teaching alone is not enough for preservice teachers to experience teaching realistically. Preservice teachers at GSU are required to complete observation/participation hours as part of their teacher training. However, it is believed that education majors should experience the real world of teaching and learning in addition to merely observing.

In interviews conducted with administrators and master teachers across the state of Louisiana, many of them confided that they were having problems with many first-year teachers. The administrators and master teachers discovered that the first-year teachers were skilled in educational theory, but lacked the ability to apply those theories adequately. It was also noted that the beginning teachers were having difficulty meeting the expectations of the administrators and master teachers interviewed.

In an effort to address these concerns and enhance teacher preparation, preservice teachers at GSU are exposed to the components of lesson planning and to the various types of lesson plans. They are required to write lesson plans in the content areas that they are going to teach and submit lesson plans for all practice lessons taught. The preservice teachers also are required which lesson plans are best suited to meet the needs of different types of learners. Preservice teachers are made aware of the importance of getting the whole class involved in the learning process. They are

238

also learn the importance of visual images and critical thinking in strengthening the teaching and learning process.

One such clinical experience provided to preservice teachers is the Natchitoches Project, an ongoing program that originated as a collaborative process between Mr. John Simon, Assistant Principal, Natchitoches Jr. High School and Grambling State University. This program provides preservice teachers an opportunity to plan and implement literacy lessons at Natchitoches Jr. High School and Cloutierville Elementary in Natchitoches, LA. The focus of this program is to afford preservice teachers with authentic, realistic clinical experiences in a public school setting.

The purpose of the clinical experiences provided to preservice teachers at GSU is to help future teachers to make the connection between pedagogy and practical experience. These experiences encourage preservice teachers to transfer theory into practice, as well as having preservice teacher examine their own classroom action and perception about the teaching profession. The preservice teachers at GSU are expected to focus not only on skills and knowledge outcomes, but also on practices reflecting professional discourse. Preservice teachers who receive an increase amount of clinical experiences will be better prepared to adjust to the complex realities of today's schools.

239

References

Dewey, J. (1916). Democracy and education. New York: Free Press.

Dewey, J. (1938). Experience and education. New York: Macmillan.

CHAPTER 20

An Analysis of Teacher Behavior and Its Effect
On the Classroom Performance and Social Behavior
Of African American Inner-City Students

Ordia L. Gee, Ph. D.
Professor of Education
Department of Special Education
Southern University
Baton Rouge, LA

INTRODUCTION

Traditionally, many parents have looked upon educational institutions with respect, trust and as a source of survival. Socially and academically, they have attempted to give their children positive support or reinforcement and, in turn, received positive responses from their children. Many parents, however, are finding themselves asking what happens to their children who are emotionally, physically, and mentally healthy from birth to age five but for reasons yet to be explored, are labeled "low achievers", "mildly retarded", "unmotivated", and so on, after entering school.

The concerns of these parents are synonymous with those of the writer. While working as a special education teacher and as an educational diagnostician on a multi-disciplinary team, it was noted that the majority of students

241

who experienced problems in both private and public schools were referred for testing when they reached third or fourth grade. These students were generally referred for special education placement by their classroom teachers for such reasons as: "they are totally unmotivated to learn", "they are in a world of their own", "they cannot keep up", "they cannot learn". Additionally, informal discussions with students in the individual testing situation yielded interesting results. When asked how they felt about their academic performance, the students' responses were usually negative.

Frequently, when students were referred for testing and/or remedial intervention, allegations on teacher referral forms did not hold true. Often, with little initial encouragement from the examiner or different teachers, these students were, indeed, eager to learn and performed well in both individual testing sessions and group teaching sessions. At other times some of the students appeared extremely "turned off" in the initial stages of the testing and remedial teaching sessions. Interest, however, was increased to a significant degree by encouragement, smiles, a pat on the back, and/or praise from the examiner or remedial teacher, resulting in progressively more positive behaviors and responses by the students.

Involvement with students through teacher-student interaction in the classroom and student-examiner interaction in testing situations prompted a desire to explore conditions

242

in the learning environment, over which students may have limited control. It was hypothesized that those conditions contribute to failure. When attempting to explore external factors which may affect student behavior and classroom performance, it is only reasonable and natural to begin by closely examining the behavior of those persons with whom the student most frequently interacts. It is usually those same persons who determine whether the student has reached or is capable of reaching desired behavioral and/or educational goals.

Research which has examined the variety of verbal and nonverbal behaviors by teachers and students as they spontaneously manifest and interact in the classroom is quite limited. Analysis of an individual classroom and the activities and interactions of a specific group of students with a single teacher is especially important if one's goal is to optimize the learning environment. Specific effects of both verbal and nonverbal teacher behaviors require identification, isolation, and examination. This assertion is based on the fact that the classroom situation is largely defined and mediated by the form and quality of interpersonal relations of the teacher and students behaving within it.

PURPOSE OF THE STUDY

Teacher-student relationships and the dynamics of interaction between the teacher and students are far from uniform. For any student within the classroom, variations in the experience of success and failure, praise or ridicule, freedom or control, autonomy or docility may have significant effects on the student's motivation and classroom behaviors. The purpose of this investigation was to observe and to quantify some in-class teacher-student behavior to determine what effects a teacher's belief systems, as expressed through the teacher's nonverbal behavior, may have on students' social behavior and classroom performance. The frequent and consistent use of strong verbal statements directed by the teacher toward students in the classroom was a significant variable that demanded attention. Therefore, the focus of the study shifted to include an analysis of teacher verbal and nonverbal behaviors.

SUBJECTS

The Students. The subjects comprising the population for the present study included 29 African-American students who were assigned to a combination fourth and fifth-grade classroom. Of the 29 subjects, 19 were fourth-graders who were new to their present teacher and two who were new to both the teacher and the school. The remaining 10 subjects were fifth-graders who had been students of the present teacher while attending fourth grade the previous year. These fifth-graders, who remained with the present teacher for another year, received a social promotion to fifth-grade. They were reported by the teacher to have been the slowest students in her class the previous year.

When the current school year began, there were too many fifth-graders for one fifth-grade class but not enough students for two classes. The same problem was encountered with fourth-graders, which resulted in one full fourth-grade class and one full fifth-grade class being assigned to two other teachers and the present teacher being assigned a combination fourth-fifth-grade classroom.

The total group of subjects consisted of 15 males (seven of whom were fifth-graders) and 14 females (three of whom were fifth-graders). The students ranged in age from 9 to 12, with the fourth-graders having an average age of 9.5, while the fifth-graders average age was 11.5. In terms of reading ability, the average reading score obtained by the fourth-graders on the Iowa Test of Basic Skills at the end of third grade was 5.3 (5th grade-3rd month). The average score obtained by the fifth-graders on the same test at the end

245

of fourth grade was 3.2 (3rd grade-2nd month). According to test scores obtained by these subjects on the Iowa Test of Basic Skills, the younger fourth-grade students were higher achievers. IQ scores obtained on group intelligence tests indicated that all of the fourth and fifth-graders obtained scores that fell within the normal range, between 90-110.

The Teacher. The teacher was an African-American female, approximately 43 years of age. She had alternately served as a fourth-grade or fifth-grade teacher for 15 years in the public schools of a large inner-city school system.

PROCEDURE

Phase 1: Teacher-student interaction was observed and recorded in 3 1/2 to 4-hour sessions for a period of 30 days. A continuous handwritten account was taken of classroom interactions and activities as they occurred (i.e., detailed descriptions of everyday classroom events and activities were simply recorded).

Phase 2: Daily recordings of teacher behaviors and student behaviors were analyzed to determine patterns of teacher behavior and to determine if patterns of behaviors developed among individual students and/or groups of students in response to teacher behaviors directed toward them.

Phase 3:   The teacher was interviewed in order to elicit information relative to students in the class and to gain some insight regarding the teacher's attitudes toward and expectations of the students.

SPELLING WITH THE FIFTH-GRADERS

9:45   The same procedure for collecting papers and initiating the formal spelling lesson utilized with the fourth-graders was duplicated with the fifth-graders. Again, it was observed that Mrs. Jones consistently read the sentence to the children but forgot to inform them of the words that they were expected to spell. Therefore, she was constantly requested by this group of children to repeat words or sentences as well as reminded by them to call the words that she wanted them to spell.

Some teacher-pupil interaction during the spelling period, however, was unique to this particular group of children. Several children from the group of fifth-graders asked, "Can we write our own sentences that would have our spelling words in them every Monday; and then you use our sentences to call the spelling words on Friday?" Mrs. Jones paused and appeared to have been giving the question some

247

thought. Before she could respond, Calvin (another fifth-grader) said, "We could even put adjectives and nouns in our sentences plus our new spelling words." Mrs. Jones responded with the following comment: "Remind me on Monday and I'll let you make up your own sentences, if you don't write sentences that sound too stupid like you usually do."

Many teacher verbal behaviors directed toward fifth-grade students did not occur during teacher directed spelling activities with the fourth-graders. Again, the relationship between teacher expectations and teacher behavior directed toward specific students were reflected in Mrs. Jones' verbal and nonverbal expressions. The following events recorded in the field notes support this assertion:

Mrs. Jones sits at the front of the classroom directly in front of the fifth-graders in rows four and five.

Mrs. Jones, "How many people studied?"

All of the students raise their hands.

Mrs. Jones, "All of you know that you haven't studied a thing. You'll flunk this test just as you always do. Frank (a fifth-grader who seldom interacts with other students in the classroom), you will probably do alright though."

248

Mrs. Jones looks at Paul (a fifth-grader who is extremely popular with other fifth-graders but who performs poorly academically). She frowns and shakes her head, appearing to indicate that she doesn't believe he will perform well on the spelling quiz.

Paul, "I did study hard at home and I'm going to make 100 on my test today."

Mrs. Jones, "Honey, I know you won't make 100 on these words today."

Paul shifts his attention from Mrs. Jones.

Mrs. Jones reads the first sentence...

...Mrs. Jones, "How many children are ready to go on?" (Asking whether the students are ready for her to dictate the next spelling word).

All of the fifth-graders, with the exception of Frank and Paul, raise their hands.

Mrs. Jones looks at Paul, curls her bottom lip, frowns, and waits a few seconds.

Mrs. Jones (looking at Paul), "Are you ready now?"

Paul, "Yes."
Mrs. Jones, "Then you should have told me, stupid, instead of having me stand here and wait."

Mrs. Jones then reads the next sentence...

Similar teacher behavior was not observed when Frank and Calvin requested that Mrs. Jones repeat a word and wait for their

written responses. An example of such an event is described below:

...Frank, "Will you say the last word again? I can't understand what you're saying."

Mrs. Jones, "Would you like for me to repeat it, baby?"

Frank nods affirmatively and she repeats the word. She then waits a few seconds.

Mrs. Jones, "How many people still are not ready?"

Frank and Calvin raise their hands.

Mrs. Jones looks at Frank.

Mrs. Jones, "I'm sorry, baby, go on." (Motions to Frank to go ahead and finish writing.)

Mrs. Jones, "Frank, I'm sorry, baby, but at this time I must go on."

Mrs. Jones starts to go on to the next word but looks

at Frank and Calvin who are still writing.

Mrs. Jones (smiling at Frank), "You're not ready."
She waits a few more seconds until they are finished.

RESULTS

An analysis of data collected from classroom
observations and teacher interviews revealed the following:

1. Overall, Mrs. Jones gave high priority to students' scores obtained on formal standardized tests of reading (Iowa Test of Basic Skills) and general intellectual functioning and to students' behavior that was indicative of what she perceived as acceptable behavior.

2. Students who performed below Mrs. Jones' expectancy level or inconsistent with teacher norms were accorded differential treatment by Mrs. Jones. They were afforded less opportunities to work in close physical proximity to Mrs. Jones and more negative teacher behavior was directed toward these students.

3. Attempts by fourth-grade students to gain Mrs. Jones' approval, to meet her expectations, and to adhere to her norms, resulted in limited positive interaction and cooperative learning activities between the fourth-grade students.

4. Fourth-graders who were frequent recipients

251

of negative teacher behaviors often exhibited signs of psychological or emotional stress (i.e., crying, lowering their heads to avoid eye contact with others, placing their heads on the desk, and so on)and disassociated themselves from the task at hand.

5.   Negative behaviors communicated by Mrs. Jones toward select students guided other students in the fourth-grade group to behave toward these students in a manner which tended to duplicate that of Mrs. Jones. Targeted students tended to cry, withdraw from activities, and/or sit staring into space in response to their peers behavior. In a sense, they became the classroom's "silent minority", constantly accepting abuse without retaliation and struggling to live up to norms imposed upon them by Mrs. Jones and significant members of the fourth-grade group.

6.   Gaining/maintaining peer approval/support appeared equally or perhaps more important than gaining Mrs. Jones' support on the part of the fifth-graders, resulting in more positive interaction and cooperative activities between fifth-graders, as compared to fourth-graders.

7.   Fifth-graders, who were frequently targets of negative teacher behavior, mobilized against such negative treatment by forming a cohesive subgroup in which members offered one another support and shared acceptance of,

252

and preference for, certain ways of behaving.

8.   The overt behavior of fifth-graders did not indicate that Mrs. Jones' negative behavior toward them had deflated their egos and self-concept, as compared to overt behaviors exhibited by fourth-graders who were recipients of frequent negative teacher behavior. However, both groups of students appeared less motivated to perform academic tasks and received poorer grades than other students in the class.

THE STUDENTS' SUBSYSTEMS

The students were not indifferent to the teacher's behaviors directed towards them. However, they did not respond as a homogeneous unit. The type of response a student made was highly dependent upon whether membership was in the fifth-grade or fourth-grade group. George Homan's (1950) conceptual scheme of persons and three elements of their behavior - "activity, interaction, sentiment" - served as lenses to assist in drawing hypotheses that may apply to the observed social behavior of students comprising this target population.

The Fourth-Graders. Students comprising the group of fourth-graders did not frequently interact (i.e., engage in verbal conversation or any form of association with peers). Little conversation or sharing of materials transpired among members of the group of fourth-graders. They adhered strongly to the teacher's rule which she constantly reminded them of: "No one talks in my class without permission unless it's me." It was apparent that they (fourth-graders) were quite conscientious about conforming to teacher norms (i.e., statements of what they were expected to do, ought to do, must do if they were to be rewarded rather than punished). Mrs. Jones reported (in her words) that "these children (fourth-graders) are more afraid of me and try to please me more than the fifth-graders, therefore, I have fewer problems in getting them to do what I want them to do." During seatwork periods when fourth-graders had completed their work, they often sat idle and stared into space or watched Mrs. Jones until she completed grading papers and initiated another activity. They seldom seized this opportunity to interact with one another. Only on three occasions were members of the fourth-grade group observed interacting (i.e., Renee and Cynthia, once; and Bob and David, twice), and those interactive activities lasted for an extremely short duration.

The fourth-graders who were constantly referred to by Mrs. Jones as her "100 students", belittled and ridiculed other members of their group for whom the teacher did not hold such high esteem. However, not one time during the observational period was this situation observed to be reversed. Thus, it appeared that the students held in low esteem by Mrs. Jones were eventually regarded in a similar vein by their fourth-grade peers, compounding the problems for these students. Silberman (1969) addressed this issue in his studies of teacher-student interpersonal relationship and concluded that many negative nonverbal teacher behaviors aimed at individual students or groups of students are visible to other students as well. Therefore, these actions not only serve to communicate to students the regard in which they are held by the teachers, but they also guide the perception of, and behavior toward, these students by their peers. Reactions exhibited by those students in Mrs. Jones' classroom towards whom negative peer behavior was directed frequently included weeping followed by psychological withdrawal.

The teacher selected group of higher status students among the fourth-graders, seeking solidarity and closeness with Mrs. Jones, often verbally encouraged and reinforced the teacher's negative behavior directed towards both members of their own groups as well as other students in the class. For example, Mrs. Jones assigned seatwork to the fourth-graders. David and Bob, two high achieving fourth-graders, asked Mrs. Jones if she would "read everybody's score out loud" and "call the names of the students who would go into the 'dummy circle'", as a result of poor performance on the assigned tasks. Mrs. Jones responded positively to their request. David looked toward Regina, a lower-achieving fourth-grader who is often reprimanded by the teacher, laughed and pointed a finger at her.

Similar repeated behaviors, such as those cited in the preceding paragraph, by members of the group of fourth-graders were observed and recorded. Little overt expressions of sentiment (e.g., affection, intimate sympathy) were shown by members of this group towards other members of the group who were targets of ridicule and scorn. When Mrs. Jones yelled at a member of the fourth-grade group, other fourth-graders offered little moral or verbal support to that member, even when they seemed aware that the teacher's treatment of the student was not justifiable. Homans (1950, p. 133), describing the relationship between interaction and sentiment among group members comprising the population for his study, found that "the more frequently persons interact with one another, the stronger their sentiments of friendship for one another are apt to be." One might conclude that, among the group of fourth-graders in the present study, lack of interaction among members of this group was accompanied by a decrease in support and sentiments of liking among them.

Derogatory statements directed by students whom Mrs. Jones held in high regard were restricted to students whom she held in low regard within their own fourth-grade group; not once was any member of the fourth-grade group observed belittling or ridiculing a fifth-grade student. However, fourth-graders did not interact with students outside their own group. A fourth-grader was never observed initiating a conversation or visiting with a fifth-grader. When attempts were made by fifth-graders to initiate any type of interaction with fourth-graders, the outcomes

were not positive. An example of such an attempt is described below:

> On several occasions when a fourth-grader came to use the pencil sharpener (at the window), a fifth-grader attempted to initiate conversation but was reprimanded by Mrs. Jones for making such attempts.
>
> David (fourth-grader and "100 student") stands and sharpens his pencil. Gregg and Paul (fifth-graders, who are seated next to each other), motion for David to come to them. Mrs. Jones looks in the direction of the three boys. Mrs. Jones says, "Lil boy, finish

sharpening your pencil and come back over here where you belong." Mrs. Jones looks at Gregg and Paul and yells, "Don't bother these people (fourth-graders) when they come over there (i.e., to sharpen their pencils). They don't want to hear any of the stupid things you probably have to say. Honey, I'm sure there's nothing you can tell these kids that they don't already know."...

There may have been an element of friendliness in the feelings of the fourth-graders towards fifth-graders, but there existed an element of constraint which seemed to have derived from the authority Mrs. Jones chose to exercise over the students. It appeared that the interaction and feelings of sentiment between members of the two groups, instead of increasing, continued to decrease since they were held closely to the amount strictly dictated by Mrs. Jones.

CONCLUSIONS AND DISCUSSION

Findings from the present study have serious implications for education. Teachers themselves, consciously and/or unconsciously, may lay the groundwork for classroom disciplinary problems and student alienation. Both the school and the school district in which the present study occurred were plagued with student disciplinary problems, vandalism, student truancy and drop-out problems, and negative publicity relative to students' standardized test

258

scores. However, in spite of the frequent negative teacher behaviors directed toward them, the low-achieving fourth and fifth-graders in Mrs. Jones' classroom did not pose serious disciplinary problems for her (e.g., classroom disruptions, talking out behavior, physical altercations, verbal power struggles with the teacher, etc.).

Brophy (1986, 1988) in his research studies linking teacher behavior with student achievement concluded that the key to enhancing school performance of low achievers is maximizing the time that they spend being actively instructed or supervised by their teachers and development of effective teaching behaviors. After having assignments returned to them by Mrs. Jones, the fifth-graders generally repeated the work with little, if any, supportive teacher assistance. In fact, Mrs. Jones seldom followed up to determine if the assignments were completed. Such positive behaviors on the part of these students tend to imply that they maintained some desire to meet the requirements of the school environment, and, that they had not, yet, completely disassociated themselves from school and learning.

The observer noted that a great deal of the fifth-graders' energy was usurped by their efforts to work out a system of behaving which would minimize confrontations with Mrs. Jones, but at the same time allow them some degree of personal satisfaction in performing selected classroom activities. The students held in low esteem by Mrs. Jones attempted to keep their activities as quiet and inconspicuous as possible so as not to disturb other students with whom Mrs. Jones was working, as well as to avoid negative attention from Mrs. Jones herself. One can only speculate about how long student motivation and commitment to learning will persist in an educational environment in which the specific student and/or groups of students are not made to feel emotionally and psychologically secure. Learning environments similar to the one observed and described in the present study may serve as precursors to student alienation, poor student performance, over-representation of inner-city students in special education classrooms, and student violence in inner-city schools?

Mrs. Jones' behavior tended to communicate the general regard she held toward all of the students. When students enter school for the first time (i.e., kindergarten), they are taught to, first, recognize their own name prior to attempting to learn other words. Educators stress the fact that focusing on the "self" communicates to students the significance of positive self-concepts and self-worth.

Students in the classroom under investigation were constantly referred to by Mrs. Jones as "lil girl" and "lil boy", often leaving the students confused about who the teacher expected to respond. After three months of school, Mrs. Jones reported that she had not yet learned the majority of her students' names, offering the explanation that she "just could not remember names." Depersonalization as reflected by failure to learn the names of students and to address them by name may be interpreted by the students as a reflection of the teacher's perception of their self-worth or the lack thereof. It would appear that students who have remained with Mrs. Jones for at least six hours a day over a period of three months and, yet, cannot be personally addressed by her would question their "worthiness" beyond that of pleasing Mrs. Jones.

A question which frequently surfaces in teacher effect studies centers around whether the teacher's behaviors cause students to respond in negative ways or whether negative student behaviors trigger negative behaviors from the teacher (i.e., "which comes first, the chicken or the egg"?). One may consider this question in terms of Mrs. Jones' prior experiences with the group of fifth-graders: What could the group of fifth-graders possibly have done the previous year to cause the teacher's negative behaviors? How much of the blame should these students assume for negative teacher responses directed towards them? A major factor which deserves consideration when responding to such a question is the fact that the fourth and fifth-graders in the present study are minors. They are also required to attend school and to make continuous adjustments and readjustments to various adult authority figures (e.g., teachers) and to a variety of curriculum materials and teaching methodologies, without having the benefit of specific formal training in making such adjustments.

In contrast to students, teachers are (and, if not, should be) the recipients of intensive teacher preparation training, which should prepare them to deal effectively with a wide range of students and ability levels. The data analysis from the present study indicate a dire need for such training. The pragmatic soundness of combining a group of fifth-grade low-achievers with a group of high-achieving fourth-graders is questionable. An implicit assumption on the part of the school decision-makers was that Mrs. Jones possessed the capability to, and would, effectively address the needs of all the students in this type learning environment. If it is common practice to combine grade levels in this fashion, more diligent efforts are required to better prepare teachers to meet the challenge of successfully addressing group, as well as individual, needs of students.

262

Teachers are expected to make the knowledge and skills acquired through teacher preparation programs applicable to classroom learning environments. As a result of their educational training, teachers are expected to exhibit keen skills in effectively changing negative student behavior (i.e., poor academic performance) to more positive behavior without posing a threat to the students' emotional and psychological comfort zones.

In conclusion, findings from the present study tend to imply an urgent need for teacher preparation programs to focus more attention on assisting prospective teachers, as well as in-service teachers, in recognizing the significance of their feelings which they express to students, verbally or nonverbally and consciously or unconsciously. Additionally, courses and numerous other opportunities should be provided for teachers to engage in teacher self-evaluation in order to void and/or minimize the carrying over of their own internal values and expectations to students in their classrooms, especially if such values result in the expression of negatively toned feelings toward students. It is also crucial that prospective teachers are afforded these opportunities early in the teacher preparation program, as opposed to providing such opportunities during their senior year. Early exposure to this type of training will allow time for teacher intervention services, where necessary. Those

263

prospective teachers who cannot profit from intervention may be guided into other more appropriate career areas without sacrificing too much time from their college program. Teacher preparation programs have a responsibility to produce teachers who provide a high quality of instruction to students and at the same time remain sensitive to the students' emotional and psychological needs.

References

Babab, E., Bernieri, F., and Rosenthal, R. (1991). Students as judge of teacher verbal and nonverbal behavior. <u>American Educational Research Journal, 28 (1)</u>, 211-234.

Beez, W. V. (1970). Influence of biased psychological reports on teacher behavior and pupil performance. <u>Learning in Social Settings</u>, eds. M. W. Miles and W. W. Charters, Jr. Boston: Allyn and Bacon, Inc.

Brophy, J. (1986). Teacher influences on student achievement, Special Issues: Psychological science and education. <u>American Psychologist, 41 (10)</u>, 1069-1077.

Brophy, J. (1988). Teacher influences on student achievement: Potential implications for instruction of Chapter 1 students. <u>Educational Psychologist, 23 (3)</u>, 235-286.

Brophy, J. and Good, T. L. (1970). Teachers communication of differential expectations for children's classroom performance: Some behavioral data. <u>Journal of Educational Psychology, 61</u>, 365-374.

Galloway, C. (1977). Interpersonal relations and education: In theory into practice. The <u>Education Digest, 42</u>, 43-44.

Garner, J. and Bing, M. (1973). The elusiveness of Pygmallion and differences in teacher-pupil contacts. Interchange, 4, 34-42.

Homans, G. (1950). Elementary Forms of Social Behavior, New York: Harcourt Brace Jovanovich.

Meichenbaum, D. H.; Bowers, K. and Ross, R. (1969). A behavioral analysis of the teacher expectancy effect. Journal of Personality and Social Psychology, 13, 306-313.

Quay, L. C. and Jarrett, O. S. (1986). Teachers' interaction s with middle and lower SES pre-school boys and girls. Journal of Educational Psychology, 78 (6), 495-498.

Richey, H. and Richey, M. (1978). Nonverbal behavior in the classroom. Psychology in the Schools, 15, 571-576.

Rist, R. (1970). Student social class and teacher expectations: the self-fulfilling prophecy in ghetto education. Harvard Educational Review, 40, 411-451.

Rosenthal, R. (1964). Experimental outcome orientation and the results of the psychological experiment. Psychological Bulletin, 61, 405-412.

Rosenthal, R. (1966). Experimenter Effects in Behavioral Research. New York: Appleton-Century-Crofts.

Rosenthal, R. (1967). Covert Communication in the psychological experiment. Psychological Bulletin, 67, 356-367.

Rosenthal, R. (1973). The Pygmalion effect lives. Psychology Today, 7, 56-63.

Rosenthal, R. and Jacobson, L. (1968). Pygmalion in the Classroom. New York: Holt, Rinehart, and Winston.

Rubovits, P. and Maehr, M. (1971). Pygmalion analyzed: Toward an explanation of the Rosenthal-Jacobson findings. Journal of Personality and Social Psychology. 19, 197-203.

Silberman, M. L. (2969). Behavioral expression of teacher's attitudes toward elementary school students. Journal of Educational Psychology, 60, 402-407.

Sommers, R. (1969). Personal Space. Englewood Cliffs, New Jersey: Prentice-Hall.

INDEX

DEVELOPING LITERACY SKILLS ACROSS THE CURRICULUM

ANNOTATED CHAPTER INDEX

CHAPTER INDEX

This chapter is designed to demonstrate that academic achievement can be enhanced greatly if literacy skills and activities are promoted throughout the educational continuum. The chapter uses a large, urban public school system as the experiential base to discuss activities and strategies that promote achievement from K - 12. It will describe creative methods that promote literacy skills and develop positive attitudes for reading and writing. The authors will also discuss the challenge of promoting literacy in higher education institutions. The task of educators, then, is to attempt to meet the challenge, overcome obstacles and create a positive teaching/learning environment that will motivate students to their highest level of excellence.

This chapter provides a definition and context for the concept of whole-language instruction. The whole-language approach to teaching reading is discussed and documentation is provided as to how students are positively impacted when reading stories about people from similar ethnic backgrounds and participating in activities that afford them opportunities to reflect and share their individual experiences. Sample lessons and literature using this approach will also be included.

How many times have you heard a student say, "I hate math"? This statement is often made by students in all levels of school, inclusive of college students. Many times students in the lower grades fail to grasp the fundamentals of math. While teaching middle school math, the author discovered that students who expressed a "dislike" or "hate" for math lacked experiences with the phase of science called "success". What was implemented within the classroom that changed "hating" math to "liking" math? In this chapter the teacher explains some strategies that were instrumental to this change in perception.

Science education has been of great concern in the United States for more than one hundred years. Committees and national level panels have called repeatedly for updating the science curriculum; more "hands-on" approaches; attention to our environment; emphasis on scientific literacy and the processes of science; and other familiar reforms. Approximately every two decades, a reform movement sparks the public interest and promotes changes in the science classroom and in how science is taught. The author of this chapter presents several science education reforms.

Cooperative learning offers a "plus" to the middle school science program. Cooperative learning is an attractive instructional format because it enables students to learn from each other, in general, and from high ability students, in particular. It offers an alternative to competitive learning which is disadvantageous to slower students and to students who have become "turned off" to school. According to David and Roger Johnson, cooperative learning environments are superior to competitive or individualistic ones for fostering learning, self-esteem, and positive attitudes toward school and classmates. In this chapter, the author shares the results of cooperative learning in an eighth grade science class.

As an educator seeking to eradicate illiteracy, the author found a marvelous means: having students write and publish their own books. According to the literature on reading and motivation, students increase engaged time and retain and apply more knowledge when learning activities are active and relevant to their lives. In this chapter an explanation is given of the rationale for and the use of student-produced books as a strategy to enhance students' literacy skill development.

"I don't like to read." "I don't want to read." "I can't read that!" The easy thing for teachers to do is to ignore students such as those with negative attitudes and focus our energy on teaching those who want to read and want to learn. A characteristic, however, of "true" teachers is that they do not ignore any student. We accept the challenge of finding those "tried and true" methods of teaching that can change a student's mind about disliking reading. Throughout the next few pages the author will share some methods that were used to help students develop a love for reading.

Literacy skills that empower students result from more than a basic literacy campaign. Critical pedagogy is necessary to prepare students to be their own agents for social change, their own creators of democratic culture. This chapter is based on an inquiry into what happened when an approach to developing critical thinking as an integral part of an aesthetic education curriculum was implemented and then revisited a decade later. The researchers investigated ways by which teaching behavior empowers or cripples students with respect to critical thinking--questioning and transforming their social world.

Community Coordinating Council, Incorporated, a non-profit organization providing educational and cultural enrichment experiences for youth and senior citizens, was organized in July of 1997. The goal is to become one of Louisiana's premiere service-oriented organizations helping to improve the quality of life for citizens in a particular area. The philosophy of the agency is that a community can be transformed when all the available resources collaborate to make a positive difference. An enormous amount of time and effort is spent coordinating and planning various experiences that support the literacy efforts of the school. The literacy-supporting activities are described in this chapter.

This chapter includes specific experiences and activities that parents can use at home to develop and reinforce literacy skills. The exercises are practical and fun for parents to use with students. According to the author the best way to ensure that a child will develop into a life-long reader is to instill in the child a love of words and a love for literature. Research has shown a strong connection between language development and learning to read. If a child understands what is said and can express thoughts effectively to others then he or she has a head start in reading. A child who has not been exposed to a wide variety of words will experience difficulty with understanding words in print.

School and business partnerships emerged over two decades ago as the result of sweeping educational reform. This collaboration began as a response to the public's outcry to improve our educational system. The landmark report, *A Nation at Risk*, emphasized the decline of academic standards and student performance in America's schools and opened a floodgate of challenges for business leaders to take a more active role in revitalizing education. This coalition has provided limitless opportunities to expand learning for students and to make learning relevant to student's lives. A description of such collaborative efforts is provided in this chapter.

A review of the literature indicates that teacher preparation programs should include diverse and consistent opportunities for students to make connections between theory and practice. As a result, the Teacher Education Department at Grambling State University provides numerous field-based experiences for students to make connections between course content and actual classroom instruction. More specifically, the Teacher Education Department was involved in a K-3 collaborative project, which involved observation-participation activities for pre-service students at an elementary school near the Grambling campus. These experiences allow students to use reflective thinking as they discuss realistic situations in the classroom.   A description of the project is presented in this chapter.

Throughout the past twenty years the author repeatedly observed numerous in-service teachers who did not sufficiently accommodate individual differences. Far too many students are unintentionally left out of activities because the teacher fails to vary methods of delivery and materials to accommodate learning styles.   An appreciation for such diversity will help teachers to experience the rewards that come from enabling each student to make his or her unique contribution to classroom life.   In this chapter various methods are presented for effectively teaching diverse populations.

This chapter focuses on some of the responsibilities schools, colleges, and departments of education must assume to prepare all teachers to teach and work with diverse student populations. Given changes in the demographic composition of the teaching force in the next decade, this chapter addresses some fundamental recommendations for revising the curriculum and structure of pre-service teacher education programs so that all teachers will be able to teach every child in any situation. If knowledge of pedagogy for teaching diverse populations has been mastered by prospective teachers, then they will be ready to link theory to practice when they begin to teach.

The purpose of this chapter is to present ways by which one teacher education program is using problem-based learning (PBL) and an integrated professional education curriculum to allow pre-service teachers to build one dynamic, inter-connected knowledge base. Emphasis is placed on teaching that crosses not only content areas, but also extends from the classes to the field experiences. This strategy increases the quality of pre-service teachers by requiring them to both learn about theories, research and practices in teaching and analyze and evaluate them. It also works to increase the number of teachers who are uniquely suited to working with an increasingly diverse student population.

Second class literacy is rampant in some communities. According to critical pedagogical advocates, this problem calls for literacy models which highlight the importance of social and cultural contexts that allow for reading the word and the world. Based on critical pedagogical approaches, a project titled "Reconstructing Lives" was created as a critical literacy approach to teaching developmental and educational psychology. The project, which is the focus of this chapter, has been used in the training of teachers and counselors, with an emphasis on student achievement.

Study skills are powerful tools for knowledge acquisition. According to developmental educators, they are especially important for maximizing "second chances" at academic growth. If study skills are to be transferable, then certain factors and conditions must be put in place. First, the transfer of study skills must be an explicit goal of instruction. Second, the learning environment should have a climate of guided and meaningful teaming strategies. Finally, learning is incomplete until it has been put to use; therefore, application is important. Details of study skills transfer are the focus of this chapter.

Often, educators reserve their high expectations and high quality schooling experiences for students who are labeled as advanced or gifted. Researchers have shown us for decades the detrimental effects of teachers' low expectations on "low or average" students. The author of this chapter believes in the ability of all students and has seen the need for positive teacher expectations, as well as a need for guidance in the learning process.   Thus a creative framework was designed titled "Mind Development, Inc. In this chapter, major components of the Mind Development, Inc. are presented.

In the teacher education program described in this chapter, clinical experiences are divided into three phases: observation, pre-service teaching, and student teaching.   Both pre-service teaching and student teaching allow the actual teaching experience to take place. Another benefit of clinical experience is gaining insight relative to the various teaching methods and learning styles. Just as in other fields of study, it is important for education majors to have clinical experiences to strengthen their abilities in the teaching profession.

CHAPTER 20: An Analysis of Teacher Behavior   241
and Its Effects on the Classroom Performance and Social
Behavior of African-American Inner-city Students

Traditionally, many parents have looked upon educational institutions with respect, trust and as a source of survival. Many parents, however, are finding themselves asking what happens to their children who are emotionally, physically, and mentally healthy from birth to age five but for are labeled "low achievers", "mildly retarded", "unmotivated", and so on, after entering school. Additionally, their children were referred for special education classes by their classroom teachers for reasons such as: "they are totally unmotivated to learn"; "they are in a world of their own"; "they cannot keep up" or "they cannot learn". When students were referred for testing and/or remedial intervention, allegations on teacher referral forms did not hold true. In this chapter, the author presents a qualitative study that gives significant insights into and solutions for such puzzling school situations.

MELLEN STUDIES IN EDUCATION